HERE'S TO YOUR GOOD HEALTH!

Drink in the all-natural
health benefits of fresh
fruit and vegetable juices with

JUICE POWER

The complete guide that
shows you how to

- Prepare fresh and natural juices at home
- Manage common health problems
- Make healthy juices a part of your life

...and much more!

JUICE POWER

CARL LOWE

Produced by The Philip Lief Group, Inc.

BERKLEY BOOKS, NEW YORK

The contents of this book are not intended to take the place of
your doctor's medical advice or supervision. Any substantial
change in regimen should be checked by your physician.

JUICE POWER

A Berkley Book / published by arrangement with
The Philip Lief Group, Inc.

PRINTING HISTORY
Berkley edition / July 1992

ISBN: 0-425-13606-X

A BERKLEY BOOK® ™ 757,375
Berkley Books are published by The Berkley Publishing Group,
200 Madison Avenue, New York, New York 10016.
The name "Berkley" and the "B" logo
are trademarks belonging to Berkley Publishing Corporation.

PRINTED IN THE UNITED STATES OF AMERICA

10 9 8 7 6 5 4 3 2 1

The publisher would like to thank Frank and Pat Campisi for their valuable contribution to this book.

CONTENTS

JUICE POWER

1

WHY SHOULD WE JUICE?

What's so important about making and drinking juice? The simple answer is that juice can improve health. Juice is part of the remedy for the poor diets that victimize so many of us.

By now, the negative effects of the Western diet on health are no secret. Nutritionists, doctors, dietitians, and even government officials warn us that too much fat, too little fiber, too few carbohydrates and too much processed food with the wrong additives are compromising our well-being. Considerable scientific evidence has shown that all the fat we eat increases our chances of developing heart disease, cancer, and other debilitating conditions.

Consequently, anyone who picks up a magazine, newspaper, or book or turns on the television has heard the nutrition news. If you want to stay healthy, the message goes, stop eating all those fatty and refined foods, get more fruits and vegetables in your juice, on your plate, and on your fork, and, oh yes, get some exercise instead of sitting there reading or listening to this message.

But many people find it's not that easy to change what they eat. Many a medical professional has found that merely explaining the health benefits of a better diet to patients does not necessarily convince them to alter lifestyles. Our taste for certain foods, our societally conditioned eating habits, the stress we encounter at our jobs, as well as the emotional satisfaction we get out of particular foods make it hard to alter our diet for health reasons. Knowing that certain foods are healthy rarely persuades us to eat them. Our emotions usually rule our palate. Sooner or later, it seems, our emotions get the food they want.

Candy-Bar Solace

Consider the solace many people get from candy bars—soft, gooey, sweet comfort that soothes. To many, a candy bar is immensely satisfying. After you've eaten your fill, licked layers of chocolate off your teeth, and satiated your need for oral delight, the high-fat content of the bar assures a long-lasting feeling of fullness. Because fat takes a relatively long time to digest, the reassuring remants of the bar sit in your alimentary canal for what may be hours as your body works to find a use for this food's oily calories.

Unfortunately, knowing that the candy bar contains unhealthy amounts of fat may delay your consumption of it, but that knowledge won't stop you from eventually cramming it into your mouth. At your initial urge to down a bar, you may hold back from eating because you believe the bar is "bad" for adults, children, and other living things. But eventually, most of us give in. Stress, fatigue, or boredom lead us to eat it.

Luckily for all of us, juice provides a way out of this nutritional dead end. Juice satisfies the same needs that lead us to eat things like candy bars. Healthy food doesn't have to be unsatisfying—the sumptuous taste of fresh juice proves this.

That's why, if you are truly interested in improving your health by improving the mix of nutrients you consume, your battle for a better diet can be aided by juicing. Juicing—the simple process of making drinks out of fruits and vegetables—is an easy way to add vitamins, minerals, and other nutrients to your diet. You'll find that juicing is fun, it's easy, it produces drinks and foods that taste wonderful, and it brings you a big step closer to the kind of diet most health experts recommend. The same desire for oral satisfaction that draws you to candy and creamy desserts can help increase your thirst for healthy, nutritious juices.

Amazing Claims

As you can see, juicing offers easy-to-prepare drinks that taste great and are good for you. That's the reason why, in the past, extravagant claims have been made for juicing. Even before scientific research proved that a diet high in fruits and vegetables was beneficial, many people advocated juicing because it takes us closer to the primitive diet human beings evolved on.

Originally, the nutritional argument for juicing was based more on intuition and personal experience than established scientific evidence. Proponents of a "primitive" diet of raw foods claimed that such meals are the ones human beings, because of their physiological history as hunters and gatherers, are "meant" to consume. Such a diet is healthier because it includes the nutrients, in raw form, that the human body was built to digest. From this perspective, the promoters of juicing denigrated cooked and refined food, claiming that processing raw food alters its pristine nutrients (rendering them harmful). They also argued that heating food completely eliminates particular nutrients that our bodies need to function properly.

Interestingly enough, many of these claims have been supported by recent research. For instance, archaeological excavations have conclusively shown that the diet of primitive man differed greatly from our own. Of course, the mere fact that primitive diets varied from what we buy in the supermarket doesn't guarantee that the old foods were better for us. But now there is considerable evidence that the refined diet prevalent in today's society has had dire consequences.

For one thing, the meat eaten by primitive people was a lot less fatty than the items that sit within plastic and Styrofoam in the meat department of today's grocery. The wild animals caught and eaten by ancient hunters were leaner than today's cattle, which are fattened before being slaughtered and cut up for consumer consumption. There is also some evidence to suggest that the kind of fat that was on those animals didn't have the same negative health consequences for humans that the fat on today's hamburger has for us. Those ancient animals contained a relatively large amount of unsaturated fat. Today's sedentary cattle are filled with saturated fat. The excessive levels of this type of fat in today's meats have been blamed for our relatively high incidence of cardiovascular disease and certain cancers.

But it isn't merely the high level of fat that is probably causing the modern-day epidemics of these disorders. Our decrease in fruit and vegetable consumption (with their health-promoting nutrients) has hurt us, too.

Juicing allows you to do something about this degradation of humanity's diet. Using a consistent juicing program—along with other healthy foods—you can enrich your diet with precisely the nutrients that research shows can prevent, alleviate, or at least lower your chances of developing the heart disease and cancer that have plagued Western society. Added to that, if you fill up with healthy foods and juices, chances are you'll be eating less of the saturated fat and cholesterol in refined foods that may make you overweight and more prone to illness.

Vitamins, Minerals, and Mystery Nutrients

Even though the benefits of juicing and eating fruits and vegetables are very clear, some people wonder why we can't merely swallow capsules of synthesized nutrients. In other words, if we know all about the vitamins and other substances in fruits and vegetables that are good for us, why can't we eat any diet we want and take pills with the proper vitamins in them?

Superficially, this approach might seem to make sense. For instance, taking certain vitamins and minerals in pills along with a high-fat diet might be healthier than a high-fat diet without supplementary vitamins. But almost all nutrition experts agree—a healthy diet is still the most important factor in preserving good health. No amounts of vitamin pills or supplements can completely offset the effects of eating poorly. Nutrient pills might provide some slight help. But they don't provide anywhere near the health benefits of a diet incorporating juices made from fresh fruits and vegetables.

Part of the problem with taking vitamins in pill-form is the unreliability of vitamin manufacturers. At the present time, there is little regulation or testing of the vitamins that are sold in retail markets. No one knows for sure whether the labels on many of the vitamins you buy in the supermarket and pharmacy accurately reflect the amounts of nutrients that are in the pills or capsules.

Still, even if vitamin pills do contain the substances claimed on their labels, there is little scientific basis for swallowing the proportions

of vitamins and minerals in the available formulations. Since no one knows the optimal dietary amounts of nutrients such as vitamin C,
A, E, iron, etc., when a vitamin company puts
nutrients in a pill, the amounts it includes are
arbitrary. In many instances, the amounts included are more of a marketing decision than
a nutritional or scientific determination. Vitamin companies are most concerned with what
will sell. They want to offer formulations that
will move off the shelves and create cash flow.
That doesn't mean vitamin companies are dis-
honest. But, in most instances, they don't have
any more of an idea about how much of a vitamin you—as an individual—should be taking
than you do. All of us inhabit bodies with different metabolisms and different dietary needs.
It's virtually impossible for a formula sold to
large masses of people to be appropriate for
everyone who buys it.

Another factor that comes into play when
considering your vitamin and mineral needs is
the great variety of micronutrients in food that
researchers know little about. Food consists of
a wide variety of chemicals. These chemicals—
vitamins, minerals, proteins, fats, carbohydrates, etc.—come in a vast array of combina-
tions. Most of these substances are contained
in very small amounts—that's why they are
called "micro" nutrients. Researchers admit
that there are many micronutrients in food
whose functions are poorly understood. Many

have functions that are not understood at all. And it's a good bet that there are many nutrients whose very existence is still unknown. You can't get these unknown nutrients in vitamin pills.

Consider the recent history of beta carotene. Research in the last few years has confirmed the health benefits of this nutrient, the substance that gives carrots their orange color. Beta carotene is a precursor of vitamin A— when you eat foods containing beta carotene, your body can convert it into vitamin A. Beta carotene is classified as one of the antioxidants, substances researchers believe help the body both to maintain a healthy cardiovascular system and prevent cancer (more on the antioxidants in chapter 3).

Because of the exciting developments indicating beta carotene's health benefits, vitamin companies have been quick to put this nutrient into vitamin pills and market them as a high-powered antioxidant that can help keep you from getting sick. And while these pills may have health benefits (although it is not firmly established how much benefit there is in taking beta carotene in a pill), nutritionists know that beta carotene is not the only "carotene" in food. It is accompanied by other carotenes (also known as carotenoids)—substances that are all similar in chemical structure, whose role in human nutrition and health is poorly understood.

Although no one knows what our bodies do

with the other carotenoids, there is a strong possibility that these chemicals do good things for us. But if you take beta carotene in pill form, you don't get the benefit of these other chemicals. You only consume them if you eat the food that contains them.

According to Dr. Ann Grandjean, chief nutrition consultant to the United States Olympic Committee, "It's important to remember that people who take vitamin pills are not the only people taking vitamins. Every time you eat food, you get a dose of vitamins, minerals, and other nutrients."

Eating food not only gives you the benefits of these vitamins and minerals, it also conveys them to you in proportions that your body is equipped to handle in a healthy manner. While the proportions of nutrients contained in pills are cooked up by chemists in a lab, the proportions in food are in relative amounts that your body—because it has evolved as a food-eating organism—knows how to handle. Taking mega-doses of certain vitamins in pill form can interfere with your body's absorptions of other vitamins and minerals. That kind of harmful interaction is avoided when you get your vitamins in food.

Possible Weight-Loss Benefits

Another real benefit to the fruits and vegetables that go into juicing is that these kinds of foods can help you lose weight and keep it down. While the fat you eat in meats is easily converted by your body to fat on your hips, the carbohydrates in fruits and vegetables are less likely to be used to make body fat.

By weight, dietary fat, just like the fat in your body, contains more than twice as many calories as do proteins and carbohydrates. Calories are a measure of the energy in your food. A gram of protein or carbohydrate has four calories, while the same weight of fat has about nine. Generally speaking, any calories you consume in your food that are not needed to fuel exercise or metabolic processes are used to create body fat.

The body uses body fat as a reserve supply of fuel. Since our bodies are designed to fatten up when there is plenty of fatty food being eaten, today's high-calorie, high-fat diet encourages our bodies to stock up on body fat.

Researchers have found it is relatively difficult for the human body to take carbohydrate or protein calories and make them into body fat. The metabolic pathways for these processes are much less efficient than those used when dietary fat is made into body fat. It can be done and, yes, if you overeat huge quantities of fruits and vegetables, you'll get fat. But it takes considerably larger amounts of carbohydrate foods to make you fat than it takes fatty foods.

Juices, of course, are low-fat foods. When you drink your calories in juices, you are not only ingesting delicious, refreshing concoctions, you are taking in the kind of calories that have the least chance of being used to make a potbelly or thunderous thighs.

An added benefit to these beverages, in these cholesterol-obsessed days, is the lack of cholesterol in juices. Since cholesterol is made only by animals, never by plants, you will never encounter cholesterol in juice.

But, that said, it is important to remember that cholesterol is a complicated subject, which we will explore a little more closely in our section about the antioxidant substances contained in juices. Thanks to deceptive advertising by some food companies, many consumers are confused about cholesterol. It is vital to remember that in discussions of cholesterol you have to distinguish between dietary cholesterol—the cholesterol in your food—and serum cholesterol—the cholesterol that ends up in your blood. Serum cholesterol is made by your body, it is not directly transferred to your blood from your food.

While eating too much dietary cholesterol is

not good for you, it is serum cholesterol (and only certain kinds of serum cholesterol) that does bad things to your heart and cardiovascular system. In general, the more fat you eat in your diet, the greater your risk of elevated serum cholesterol and heart disease. The amount of cholesterol in your diet has a much weaker effect on your heart than does dietary fat.

In any case, the nutrients you drink in juices will probably help your heart health. It is believed that the antioxidants in fruits and vegetables limit the deposit of cholesterol on the walls of blood vessels. In addition, the fiber in these foods helps the body eliminate cholesterol. Fiber also has many other beneficial health effects, which we will explore in the next section. Contrary to what many books on juicing maintain, you should consume the fiber in the fruits and vegetables you use to make your juices. Fiber has too many great benefits to pass up.

Delicious Nutrition

All of these benefits of juicing show that foods don't have to taste like sawdust to be good for you. The clichéd notion that health foods are poor in taste and deprive you of foods that feel great in your mouth is, ironically, the opposite of the truth. And even though the modern-day palate seems to prefer soft, gooey foods drenched in fat, a diet that sticks exclusively to items like burgers, fries, onion rings, and shakes is missing the true culinary taste sensations available to us. Various juices made with different fruits and vegetables offer an astonishing spectrum of tastes. On the other hand, the junk foods beloved by so many actually convey paucity of palate sensations.

In truth, furits and vegetables are the original desserts. Their sweetness and ripe deliciousness are the tastes that human taste buds evolved to savor. Unlike the assembly-line foods that fast-food restaurants crank out with mindless consistency, fruit and vegetable juices never cease to surprise. No healthy, well-rounded diet should do without them.

2

JUICE AND FIBER

A touchy subject among juice enthusiasts is what to do with the fiber that many juicers filter out of the juice of fresh fruits and vegetables. Some well-known juice advocates believe that a chief benefit of making juice from produce is the elimination of this fiber—what they refer to as "merely" cellulose.

The cellulose they're talking about—the fiber—is the pulpy material that actually makes up the cell walls in fruits and vegetables. Fiber is the construction material that gives plants their firmness. (Animals have bones to hold their bodies together, plants have fiber.) Fiber is often referred to as the "roughage" contained in vegetarian foods.

Contrary to what some juice promoters preach, however, for the most health benefits, the fiber should be be left in the juice rather than filtered out. Or, as an alternative, it should only be partly filtered out. Some manufacturers of juicers who recognize fiber's benefit say the fiber should be filtered out and then saved to be mixed in with other foods. Fact is, there are just to many well-established health benefits to fiber to justify a program that eliminates it entirely.

Those who urge us to eliminate the fiber say that filtered juice is more palatable—an issue we'll get to later—and they hold that fiber is "difficult" to digest. According to these juice-niks, when your digestive system tries to deal with too much fiber, it tires itself out and is unable to absorb the other nutrients in the juice properly. The juice promoters who hold this position believe that the most important nutrients in juice are better digested in the absence of fiber. And some juice fanatics actually insist that fiber is bad because you often have to chew it—and that takes too much time! (Don't laugh. Some books actually make this argument.)

If you examine these antifiber arguments, you'll find that a lot of these misinformed, antifiber nutrition "experts" don't seem to understand what fiber is. Aside from the fact that it is the vegetable world's skeletal structure, fiber is, by nutritional definition, indigestible carbohydrate. It is starch that passes through your digestive system without being absorbed. Fiber is only contained in vegetarian foods. Animal foods have no fiber. No matter how chewy and tough your steak is, you'll never find any fiber in it. Gristle, yes. Fiber no.

Fiber: Just Passing Through

Just because fiber is not digested and passes through the alimentary canal practically intact does not mean it has no function in your digestive tract. Although the precise mechanisms by which it interacts with nutrients in the intestines is not well understood, fiber researchers all agree that fiber is an important component in a healthy diet—one of the most important. Lack of it can result in some serious health consequences.

Only recently have scientists begun to appreciate the vital role fiber plays in human health. As a matter of a fact, up until a few years ago, nutrition scientists' methods for measuring the fiber in foods was faulty and irrelevant to human nutrition: scientists used to dip food into acids and bases and then weigh whatever was left—the part that wasn't dissolved by the chemicals. That small amount was considered the food's "crude" fiber.

Eventually, however, researchers realized

that this meager amount of nondissolvable plant matter didn't represent anything meaningful in terms of human nutrition. The amount of fibrous material that actually passed undigested through the human intestine had little correlation with this old-fashioned acid-base test, and many foods loaded with indigestible fiber were found to have very little "crude" fiber. So, today, most nutrition experts consider a food's fiber to be "dietary" fiber, a measurement recorded in grams, which more accurately reflects the portion of vegetarian food not digested by the human digestive tract.

Many Types of Fiber

A common misconception about fiber is that it is a homogenous substance that keeps your bowel movements coming at regular intervals. In actuality, there are many different types of fiber. The components of the various fibers depend on what plant produces them. And although some experts on juicing would have you believe that all fiber is "merely'" cellulose, different fibers from various sources actually contain compounds known as pectin, lignin, hemicellulose, and other types of carbohydrates as well as cellulose. Each of these names denotes a different chemical compound with different nutritional characteristics.

The vast differences in the various fibers and the wide range of health benefits you can get from each are the main reasons why taking fiber supplements in pill form is not as healthy as consuming a wide variety of fibrous foods. As a matter of fact, that's also one of the great things about drinking different homemade juices: when you make your own juices and leave some of the fiber in, you can partake of almost all of the different fibers and get all of the protective health benefits.

Until recently, most of the publicity surrounding fiber has trumpeted its laxative benefits. While it is true that fiber frequently absorbs water as it passes through your intestines and speeds the elimination of feces, not all fiber performs this task efficaciously.

To make fiber easier to understand, nutrition experts classify fiber under two headings—water-soluble and non-water-soluble. (To make things even easier, we'll refer to these two types as soluble and insoluble.) The soluble ones—such as the pectin in apples—do not generally have a strong laxative effect. The insoluble ones—such as the cellulose in whole wheat—can soak up heroic amounts of water, and as they swell in your intestine they help you eliminate wastes.

Incidentally, the great oat-bran craze that

swept the United States during the 1980s was actually a craze for soluble fiber. At the time, a popular book on cholesterol control pointed out that the fiber in oat bran, when eaten in large quantities, could lower serum cholesterol. Because of the resultant media furor, for a while it seemed as if every food manufacturer was dumping oat bran into every food.

A factor leading to the end of the oat-bran craze was the revelation that cholesterol-lowering soluble fiber was not restricted to oats. It could be had in many foods such as prunes, pears, and grapefruit—fruits you should be drinking in your juices.

Arguments Against Fiber

Aside from health benefits, fiber is also the source of intestinal gas that can cause you embarrassment and discomfort. Although fiber is considered indigestible, some of it does partially break down during its intestinal journey. As it partially disintegrates, the bacteria in your gut convert a portion of it into gas. Some experts believe that you can reduce this flatulence by switching gradually to a high-fiber diet if you are currently eating a highly refined diet. However, it seems evident that for many people some degree of intestinal gas is a constant companion to high-fiber foods. You just have to learn to live with it.

Besides the occasional attacks of gas that accompany drinking fiber in your juice, another argument against fiber is that it decreases your absorption of nutrients. This is true. When you increase your intake of fiber, your body absorbs fewer minerals from your food. For instance, if you eat a very high fiber meal, you will probably excrete more dietary copper, iron, and zinc. Without the fiber, your body would take up more of these minerals. However, nutrition experts are divided on how significant this added excretion is. While it may raise your dietary requirements for these minerals slightly, if you are eating a healthy diet of a variety of foods, chances are you will be getting more than enough of them in your food anyway.

But some of the best news about fiber is that it takes along more than just some of your minerals as it speeds its way through the alimentary canal. It also binds harmful substances that might otherwise clog your arteries or increase your cancer risk.

Consider this: A study that looked at rural African dietary habits and digestion found that many Africans eating high-fiber meals excreted the waste products from their meals in less than half the time it took Europeans. From the time they ate, the Africans in the study spent about a day and half digesting a meal before its remains left. A comparable British study group took more than three days.

The ramifications of studies like these are important. By speeding food through the gut, fiber reduces the chances of constipation, diverticulosis, and other lower-intestine difficulties. Added to that, fiber makes it harder for your intestines to absorb carcinogens. Instead of infiltrating the intestinal walls and entering your body where they can wreak havoc, a larger portion of these carcinogens pass out with your stools. In addition, fiber also lowers the amount of fat and cholesterol that is absorbed from your meals.

And, for those concerned about their weight, as the fiber in your stomach and intestines absorbs water it makes you feel full and less likely to overeat. Plus, since it is indigestible, fiber contains zero calories. So when you drink juice with fiber, you can fill up on this bulky material and be assured that the fiber will never be converted to body fat. Only excess calories can be made into fat.

Fiber and Heart Disease

Studies in Africa, Europe, and North America have also extablished that people who eat diets high in fiber—fiber such as those you can have in your juice—suffer less heart disease than populations eating the typical, Western, low-fiber diet. One study, which examined people in Ireland, Boston, and California, found that over a period of two decades, folks who ate the highest amounts of fiber had the least incidence of heart problems.

Unfortunately, modern, refined foods seem invariably to be stripped of their fiber. In the United States the total amount of fiber in the average person's diet has dropped by more than three fourths during the past century. As fast foods, meats, refined desserts, white bread, white rice, iceberg lettuce, and other low-fiber foods have been marketed widely, people's taste for high-fiber fruits and vegetables has dropped precipitously. Along with this drop in fibrous foods, the incidence of heart disease, diabetes, and some cancers—including colon cancer—has risen astronomically. Many experts blame these epidemics at least partially on the drop in fiber consumption.

Coincidentally, it has been found that people who eat the most fiber also tend to consume the least amount of fat. So when you consume large amounts of vegetables and fruit in your drinks, you'll be cutting the fat—another important factor in minimizing your chances of developing heart disease.

As an added benefit of fiber consumption, when you do eat some fat, more of it will pass through without being absorbed. That effect, some researchers believe, can lower the levels of cholesterol in your blood. In particular, the soluble fibers—such as the pectin in apples and citrus fruits—can lower your serum cholesterol in another manner: by binding to chemicals known as bile acids.

Bile acids are manufactured by the gallbladder from the body's supply of cholesterol (the waxy material that the body makes and sends through the bloodstream). As the soluble fibers link up with these bile acids and escort them out of the body in the stool, the gallbladder has to use up more cholesterol to make still more bile acids. This extra cholesterol consumption by the gallbladder ultimately means that increased amounts of cholesterol are filtered from the blood. Consequently, your serum cholesterol decreases. So when you put that apple or orange with its pectin—a type of soluble fiber—into the juicer, what you may be doing, in effect, is pulling a tiny bit of cholesterol out of your blood vessels.

Cancer Prevention

Just as researchers have found that societies that eat a high amount of fiber usually have low incidences of heart disease, in similar fashion, epidemiological studies have shown that populations eating high-fiber diets suffer lower rates of cancer. In particular, several studies have shown that colon cancer is reduced in countries where people eat a lot of fiber. And in the lab, at least one study with rats has shown that the fiber in wheat bran and citrus fruits gave animals increased resistance to colon cancer.

Insoluble fiber seems to have the greatest protective effect against colon cancer. Bran, the fiber from whole grains, is a major source of insoluble fiber. Apples, which contain soluble fiber, also contain a fair amount of insoluble fiber. And corn, too, contains insoluble fiber.

As for breast cancer, some researchers believe a diet high in fiber may similarly alleviate the risk of this disease, although the population studies do not demonstrate this conclusively. But since this cancer, in some studies, has been linked to a high-fat diet and fiber tends to bind fat in the digestive tract, there's a good chance that a high-fiber diet does help.

Additionally, the American Diabetes Association has recommended adding fiber to the diets of diabetics. It has been found that when those suffering diabetes eat a low-fat, fiber-rich diet, their diabetes is easier to control with less medication. The association recommends consuming about forty grams of fiber daily. (An apple has about three grams, a cup of prunes has eighteen, and a cup of green peas has ten.)

An important point to remember is that when you increase your fiber intake, you should also increase the amount of water you drink. Since fiber absorbs water and takes it out of your system, extra water is necessary to keep your digestive processes running smoothly. Luckily, when you take your fiber in your juice, the water is supplied by the fruits and vegetables you are drinking.

The Taste of Fiber

Although the health benefits of fiber are numerous, some people just don't like to drink much of it in their juices. Fiber makes the juice thicker and it is bulky. That is why many juice-making machines filter the fiber out.

What should you do if you find it hard to drink your juices with the fiber?

The answer is to add small amounts of fiber to your juices to accommodate your taste while attempting to grow accustomed to having fiber in your drinks. Even if you discover that you never want to drink all of the fiber that was originally in your fruits and vegetables, just leaving a little bit in is better than none. And if you work your way to gradually drinking a little extra fiber in your drinks, you'll be going yourself a big health favor. For while juices contain many important vitamins and minerals (as we'll see), the part you don't digest—the fiber—may be one of its most important health benefits.

3

JUICE'S HEALTHY VITAMINS AND MINERALS

Even if you decide to drink your juice without a healthy dose of fiber, you'll find that juice is still the source of myriad vitamins and minerals that are crucial to well-being. Many nutrition experts agree that members of Western society not only don't drink enough liquids, but they also feel that when we do drink, we generally drink beverages that don't do us much good.

Thanks to the marketing efforts of large companies that sell soda pop and beer, these two beverages now form a considerable part of the Western world's diet. And while apologists for these beverage manufacturers point out that juice often has just as many calories (or more) than soft drinks and alcoholic beverages, they overlook the fact that juice contains important nutrients that these bottled drinks lack.

First, before we talk about vitamins and minerals or other nutrients, let's consider the issue of calories. It is true that juice contains calories in the form of sugar. It is also true that if you consume too many calories—more calories than your body burns up in exercise or metabolic processes—your body will put on extra body fat.

Consequently, some people would have you believe that sticking to diet soft drinks that have little or no sugar will help you reduce your weight. That's faulty reasoning. There is very little evidence to show that drinking diet drinks with artificial sweeteners will help you lose or keep off weight. Scientific studies have not supported this. Consumers who drink diet drinks aren't any thinner than people who drink other beverages. The soft-drink companies know this even if they don't come out and say it. And if you read the advertising for their diet beverages carefully, you'll find that the manufacturers never claim their products will help you lose weight. They tiptoe around this issue by implying that drinking beverages with aspartame or saccharin (artificial sweeteners) is part of a "healthy life-style." Whatever that means. It doesn't mean much.

Actually the advertising campaigns designed

to make us want to consume diet drinks are part of an expensive, flashy con game set to music and jingles. These overproduced commercials delicately suggest diet soft drinks are good for us, but they know they can't come right out and say it because it simply isn't true. If the soft-drink manufacturers made any substantial health claims for these products, the Food and Drug Administration, whose job it is to review advertising claims, would make them stop immediately. The simple truth is that these beverages are only colored water flavored by laboratory chemicals. Their massive advertising support in the media doesn't make them any healthier. It only makes them more popular. That's why consumption of soft drinks has more than tripled in the past forty years.

As for alcoholic beverages—recently some studies claim that a drink or two a day of beer or wine can help keep your serum cholesterol down. Despite these claims, if you don't drink now, you shouldn't start for the sake of your cholesterol. There are too many negative side effects of alcohol consumption to make this habit worthwhile. Alcohol adds what many people call "empty" calories to the diet that can exacerbate a weight problem. The famous beer belly is just that—extra body fat around the middle caused by consumption of beer.

Alcohol can also cause liver disease. When

the liver uses alcohol for energy, it may neglect the fat that it normally burns for fuel. And when the unused fat accumulates in the liver, it can lead to cirrhosis, a disease that is sometimes fatal.

If you are a moderate alcohol drinker now, you don't have to give it up to enjoy good health. But be cautious about accepting health claims for alcohol consumption.

And, oh yes, about the calories in juices—it is true that if you stuff yourself with juice, you run the risk of adding more body fat. The key is to drink them in moderation. Because their calories are anything but empty.

Healthy Coloring

Unlike the artificial coloring in soft drinks— nutritionally worthless chemicals put into the drinks to improve sales—much of the pigment in fruits and vegetables is actually good for you. The fruit-and-vegetable-coloring agent that's gotten the most good press lately is beta carotene. Studies show that people who have high levels of this nutrient in their body tend to have lower rates of cancer and heart disease.

Although there's been a lot of PR in the press concerning beta carotene and several vitamin

companies have rushed to market with capsules of the stuff, few people understand what
this nutrient is and how it functions.

First of all, beta carotene belongs to a family
of substances called the carotenoids. All of
these substances are pigments that give fruits
and vegetables their color. And while many nutrition researchers believe that beta carotene
is the carotenoid with the most health benefits,
chances are all of the carotenes have some function. (And you consume them all when you
drink a variety of juices. But you only get one
carotenoid—beta carotene—when you take a
beta carotene pill.)

Altogether there are more than four hundred
carotenoids that occur in vegetarian foods. A
lot remains to be discovered about this class of
nutrients that makes carrots orange and apples
red. But scientists do know that about fifty of
these nutrients are vitamin A "precursors"—
they can be made by the human body into vitamin A. Of these fifty, beta carotene is the one
carotenoid that can be made most efficiently
into vitamin A. Beta carotene is also the most
prevalent carotenoid.

One huge advantage beta carotene has over
vitamin A is its safety. Taking too much vitamin A can be dangerous. When you take large
doses of this vitamin—especially over a long
period of time—you can damage your liver.
Some people suffer vitamin-A poisoning when

they overdose on vitamin-A supplements and eat a diet filled with organ meats that are rich in vitamin A. Besides liver problems, other symptoms of what is called hypervitaminosis A include pain in your joints, thickening of your bones, hair loss, and jaundice. (And like cholesterol, vitamin A is only found in animal foods. It is not present in fruits and vegetables.)

Beta carotene, on the other hand, is almost never toxic. The body can cope with this substance in large quantities in a much safer manner than it copes with vitamin A. When foods rich in beta carotene are eaten, the body only converts some of the beta carotene into vitamin A. If the body already has enough vitamin A, it won't convert any of the beta carotene, it will merely absorb the carotenoid and store it.

If you eat extremely huge amounts of beta carotene, you may alter your skin color, but chances are you won't suffer any serious side effects. For instance, some vegetarians, who eat several carrots a day or habitually drink prodigious quantities of carrot juice, find that a portion of the excess beta carotene finds its way into their skin, endowing it with an orange hue. This may be embarrassing, but as far as anyone knows, it is not deleterious to health (although it is not recommended).

JUICE POWER

Beta Carotene Versus Villainous Oxygen

The exciting health news about beta carotene and the carotenoids started when several researchers began measuring levels of beta carotene in the diets and blood of people who had cancer and then examined people who were healthy. An article in the *Journal of Nutrition* that analyzed nine studies of diet and lung cancer found that there was "a decreased risk [of lung cancer] with increased intake of carotenoids or green or yellow-orange vegetables."

Some of these studies also found that smokers—who are at greatest risk for lung cancer—lowered their cancer risk when they ate a diet rich in beta carotene and the other carotenoids. Other studies that examined the level of beta carotene in people's blood found that those persons with the highest levels of this nutrient ran the least risk of lung cancer. They also found that smoking seemed to decrease serum beta carotene.

Still, if you do smoke, the health risks of this habit can be deadly. A study in Finland that followed more than 4,500 men for twenty years found that the smokers in the group did not seem to benefit very much from eating foods high in antioxidants. On the other hand, in this same Finnish group, the nonsmokers significantly decreased their lung-cancer risk by eating diets high in carotenoids, vitamin C, and vitamin E. The nonsmokers who ate diets lacking these nutrients were four times more likely to get cancer.

Before these studies were performed, most researchers assumed that beta carotene's health benefits derived from the fact that it was made into vitamin A in the body. However, several of the studies have demonstrated that eating a diet high in vitamin A did not have the same cancer-protective effect that consuming the carotenoids had. That has led scientists to conclude that the carotenoids do not have to be made into vitamin A to fight cancer in your body.

Why are the carotenoids so beneficial? Rather than only providing raw material for vitamin-A production, beta carotene and other carotenoids serve as antioxidants in the human body. Antioxidants form a kind of "health bomb squad," arresting and defusing harmful substances that would otherwise destroy structures within your cells.

Since oxygen is necessary to life, it seems odd that *anti*oxidants are needed in the body to keep us healthy. However, the oxygen we breathe in as air is in the form of normal oxygen—unreactive pairs of oxygen molecules.

These relatively quiescent double pairs of molecules are absorbed in the lungs by the blood and then are used in many different physiological reactions.

Within the body, however, "singlet" molecules of oxygen are released into the cells as a by-product of various metabolic processes. Left on its own, singlet oxygen is a very damaging substance. Because it is an unstable chemical that reacts with almost anything it touches, singlet oxygen can tear apart cell membranes, wreck enzymes, and destroy DNA. And the havoc doesn't stop there. According to a Vitamin Nutrition Information Service interview with Dr. Norman I. Krinsky, professor of biochemistry at the Tufts University School of Medicine, "singlet oxygen reactions can lead to the formation of 'free radicals,' another species of reactive molecules capable of causing damage to cellular components."

The molecular structures of the several different types of carotenoids—including beta carotene—are so laid out as to be able to absorb the destructive force of singlet oxygen. According to Dr. Krinsky, beta carotene has eleven chemical bonds that suck out the destructive energy of singlet oxygen and release it as harmless heat. In the process, the nasty singlet oxygen is converted to "normal" oxygen, which is much less likely to cause cellular trouble.

Beta carotene is particularly potent at de-

fusing singlet oxygen. When it is done dissi-
pating the destructive force of a molecule of
singlet oxygen, beta carotene isn't degraded
into another substance, it's ready to take care
of more. As a matter of fact, each molecule of
beta carotene can defuse about a thousand molecules of singlet oxygen.

For plants, carotenoids aren't merely a device
for enhancing color, they're a survival mechanism as well. When green plants make their
own food from sunlight—a process known as
photosynthesis—singlet oxygen is also released
within the plant cells. When this oxygen ap-
pears, the plants utilize the carotenoids to ren-
der it harmless. Without these substances,
green plants would be destroyed by singlet oxygen.

Carrot Juice Beats Cancer
and Heart Disease

It is believed that in the human body beta carotene primarily protects against cancer by
standing guard over the chromosomes within
the cell nuclei. When the chromosomes—the
genetic material that is used in cell reproduc-
tion—are damaged by singlet oxygen or other
substances called "free radicals," mutations can
take place that may lead to cancer.

Despite their name, free radicals are not political groups. They are unstable molecules that, like singlet oxygen, can react on a cellular level with other molecules to cause destroy cell structures. When metabolic processes initially release free radicals, these dangerous chemicals can spread in a chain reaction that rapidly releases larger and larger quantities of other free radicals. Unchecked, free radicals can launch devastating attacks on cell membranes—killing cells—or they can severely damage chromosomes.

The reaction of free radicals (or singlet oxygen) with other chemicals is called oxidation. Since beta carotene and other carotenoids protect membranes, chromosomes, and other structures from oxidation, they are known as antioxidants.

As Dr. Krinsky points out, the action of carotenoids against free radicals may account for "epidemiological evidence suggest[ing] that individuals whose diets are low in carotene have a greater incidence of lung, stomach, colon, prostate and cervical cancer." So, theoretically, if you drink carotene-rich juice, such as carrot juice, you may be protected from some of these diseases.

Another important benefit of carotenoids is their action against heart disease. Researchers now believe that when cholesterol builds up on the walls of arteries and causes atherosclerosis (hardening of the arteries), it is due to oxidative reactions that modify the normally harmless cholesterol.

Serum cholesterol (the cholesterol in your blood) is used by the body to manufacture various hormones—not all of the body's cholesterol ends up on artery walls. And, theoretically, if we all ate a very low fat diet, avoided stress by never getting mad at our spouses or our bosses, and ran around the block at least once an hour, hardly any of us would have hardening of the arteries or heart disease.

Be that as it may, cholesterol is shuttled around the body in the blood as part of molecules called lipoproteins. In the vernacular that has sprung up in health magazines and books, the high-density lipoproteins (HDLs) have been dubbed the "good" cholesterol and the low-density lipoproteins (LDLs) the "bad" cholesterol. What all this really means is that the cholesterol ferried about by LDLs is the stuff that ends up blocking arteries and killing people. Cholesterol in HDLs does not cause harm.

The latest research has found that the process by which LDLs clog arteries involves oxidation of the LDLs. LDLs are oxidized by coming into contact with free radicals. After the LDL is oxidized and damaged, it is attacked by immune cells (macrophages), which normally are supposed to float around the blood attacking germs and foreign cells endangering the body. Instead, the macrophages stuff themselves with LDL, until they are bulging blobs known as "foam cells." The foam cells gather on artery walls and form lesions that are the beginning of atherosclerosis. These lesions clog the cardiovascular system and can be fatal.

The Vitamin Nutrition Information Service quotes Dr. Joseph Witztum, a medical professor at the University of California who has studied the oxidation of LDL, as stating: "macrophages do not normally take up native LDL.... If oxidation can be blocked, LDL can be prevented from becoming a player in the events that lead to coronary artery disease."

As it turns out, LDL normally carries around its own supply of antioxidants to prevent oxidation from taking place. When atherosclerosis begins, researchers believe that something takes place that short-circuits LDL's antioxidant defenses, although they are not sure how this happens. But they do recommend that Americans and other citizens of Western countries that suffer a high rate of heart disease consume an increased amount of fruits and vegetables to keep the supply of antioxidants high.

Similarly, medical researchers who have studied angina—a form of heart disease characterized by chest pain—also urge a diet including plenty of fruits and vegetables high in beta carotene and vitamin C, another antioxidant.

Vitamin C—Superhero Vitamin

Just as the fruits and vegetables in juices can
be excellent sources of beta carotene and the
entire family of carotenoids, they are also rich
in the antioxidant vitamin C, ascorbic acid.

Vitamin C has had a long, rich history in the
annals of nutrition. European sailors in the
1400s and 1500s consistently suffered from
scurvy, a disease that resulted from a diet deficient in ascorbic acid. On one voyage around
Africa's Cape of Good Hope alone, the explorer
Vasco da Gama lost a hundred of his men—two
thirds of his crew— to scurvy. In the 1530s a
French expedition led by Jacques Cartier was
saved from the scourge of scurvy by Amer-
Indians living in what is now Quebec. They
showed the Europeans how to brew vitamin-C–
rich tea from the bark of the arborvitae tree.
But it wasn't until the 1700s that Dr. James
Lind, a British naval surgeon officially figured
out that ships should carry citrus fruits (excellent sources of vitamin C) and serve them to
sailors to prevent scurvy.

Strangely enough, most animals don't need
to eat foods containing vitamin C. Their bodies
make it! Humans and guinea pigs are two of
the exceptions to this rule. They, as well as fruit

bats and a few types of grasshoppers, need to eat this nutrient. Cats, dogs, cows, elephants, cockroaches, giraffes, and just about all the other animals on the face of the earth are capable of making their own ascorbic acid.

Vitamin C is rather miraculous in its versatility and safety. According to Dr. Oliver Alabaster, director of cancer research at the George Washington University Medical Center, "less than 10 milligrams per day is enough to prevent scurvy—only one five-thousandth of an ounce! Yet despite this enormous power, large doses of vitamin C are not dangerous and have never killed anyone."

When Dr. Alabaster talks about large doses of vitamin C, he is referring to pills and tablets containing the vitamin. And while it is safe to take large amounts of vitamin C in pill form, some nutrition professionals would argue that it is even safer—and preferable—to take it in your juice, which also will contain other vitamins and minerals.

But in any case, whether you take your ascorbic acid in juice or swallow pills, this versatile nutrient has an antioxidant effect similar to beta carotene—with the added benefit that large amounts of vitamin C won't turn your skin orange. Studies have shown that, like beta carotene, vitamin C fights free radicals. Several researchers have found that high levels of vitamin C in the blood protect the LDLs from oxidation and subsequent blocking of arteries.

In addition, it has been proven that vitamin C counters the carcinogenic effect of chemicals called nitrates and nitrites that are sometimes added to meat as preservatives.

But what about vitamin C's reputed protection against colds? While it has been proven that a lack of vitamin C can compromise your immune system and reduce your number of T cells (white blood cells that intercept germs), there is little proof that large amounts of it will make you less vulnerable to catching a cold. However, some studies have shown that if you do catch a cold, large doses of vitamin C will probably reduce the amount of time that you are incapacitated.

When you make your own juices at home, chances are good that they will contain substantially more vitamin C than supermarket juices. Heat, light, and exposure to air destroy this versatile vitamin. For example, orange juice, which is rich in vitamin C, is frequently pasteurized before being frozen or packaged, and this heating process wipes out a considerable portion of its ascorbic acid. Still more is destroyed during bottling or packaging. The light shining into a bottle of juice will eliminate more of the vitamin. And if the juice is stored for any length of time, an even greater quantity of vitamin C breaks down.

Also when you shop for juices at the store, be aware that not all liquids bearing the word "fruit" contain much real fruit. And many such products have absolutely no vitamin C at all. For instance, fruit "ades" such as orangeade only have to be made with 15-percent juice, fruit "drinks" with 10 percent, and lemon drinks with only 6 percent. And if the label says "fruit-flavored," then the beverage may contain less than 10-percent juice. Don't look for vitamin C—or fiber or beta carotene, for that matter—in these drinks. Most of what you get is simply sugar and water.

And as for "artificially flavored" drinks, those may contain absolutely no juice at all.

The Potassium in Juice

Another important nutrient you can get in your homemade juice is the mineral potassium—a substance that is also known as an electrolyte. Electrolytes help generate the electric impulses that are necessary for the healthy functioning of your heart. Potassium—and the other electrolytes—are also the minerals you lose when you sweat heavily. That's why the makers of sports drinks usually tout their beverages' potassium content. These food companies would have you believe that perspiration losses of potassium require exercisers to replenish the body's supply of this mineral immediately.

In almost all instances, such claims are over-

Carl Lowe

stated. When you exercise heavily and sweat profusely, your biggest immediate need is plain water. Exercisers encounter dehydration much more frequently than electrolyte problems. And no matter when you exercise, a drink of juice later in the day or in the evening will almost certainly be sufficient to resupply potassium.

That doesn't mean a diet high in potassium isn't required for good health. It does mean that a leisurely after-shower drink of juice to get your dietary potassium is preferable to a hurried gulp of overpriced sports drink during a workout.

Drinking juices high in potassium, researchers have found, is necessary for keeping blood pressure down. For, while many people have heard that the sodium in salt leads to hypertension, the truth is that it is probably the balance between both potassium and sodium that most strongly influences blood pressure.

It is thought that consuming too much sodium—often found in salty, processed foods as well as in the shaker—and too few potassium-rich foods may set the stage for hypertension. And although there are substantial amounts of potassium in beef and chicken, these foods are usually eaten with large amounts of salt that counteract potassium's benefits. These foods can also include large portions of fat. However, when you drink juices high in potassium, you avoid salt overload as well as fat. In that way, the potassium in the juice helps keep your pressure down to healthy levels.

Because of publicity in the media, many people consider bananas one of the best sources of potassium. And they are—but they are not the only place to get your potassium. Other excellent sources include oranges, tomatoes, broccoli, and cantaloupe.

A potassium point to keep in mind: Although people on diuretic blood-pressure medication sometimes take potassium pills, no one in normal health who is not under a doctor's supervision should ever do so. Diuretics flush potassium from your body, thus necessitating large doses of potassium. But large doses of potassium can disrupt the heartbeat and be fatal. You should also avoid using salt substitutes that contain potassium. For a healthy person, food is better than vitamin and mineral pills. The potassium in juice can never harm you.

And if you need another good reason to drink juice, consider the amount of phosphorus many Americans get in their diets. It may be too much for their own good.

Phosphorus is a mineral that, along with calcium, aids in forming strong teeth and bones. It also is found in the membranes surrounding cells and is a component of many important enzymes that take part in making energy from food.

Rarely does anyone in Western society develop a deficiency of phosphorus. This mineral is in our favorite foods, namely meat and soda pop. (Their high phosphorus content was one reason soft drinks used to be known as "phosphates.") If you frequent the local fast-food joint and often have a burger and cola, then you're getting plenty of phosphorus.

In terms of overall health, it's the relative proportions of nutrients that count. And just as many nutritionists believe that relative amounts of both potassium and sodium matter for keeping down blood pressure, many also feel that the proportion of both phosphorus and calcium in your diet is what keeps your bones healthy. Many of us consume less and less milk and fewer vegetables, both of which can be good sources of calcium. At the same time, soft-drink consumption has skyrocketed. So phosphorus consumption has been elevated, too.

Has our calcium consumption dropped so far in comparison to phosphorus that it will do many of us harm? No one knows for sure. But the need to keep calcium up and phosphorus down to healthy levels is another reason to get your juicer going. Juices will have the right proportions of both minerals to keep you feeling fit.

4

PREPARATION OF FRUITS AND VEGETABLES FOR JUICING

Unless you are growing your fruits and vegetables in your own organic garden, you run the
risk that the produce you are putting in your
juices has been exposed to pesticides, preservatives, and other chemicals meant to keep
food's appearance pristine. If, like most people,
you buy your fruits and vegetables in a normal
supermarket or grocery, you will occasionally
buy produce with some extraneous chemicals
on the surface or inside.

Fortunately, in most cases, only a very tiny,
probably harmless amount will remain. And
while it's disturbing that the federal govern-

ment and the food industry have decided that some consumer exposure to these chemicals is a necessary part of the modern food chain, there are easy precautions (which we'll get to in a moment) you can take to minimize risk.

Keep in mind that at the present time the regulatory agencies responsible for inspecting fruits and vegetables and keeping heavily contaminated foods off the shelves do allow a certain level of pesticides—albeit small—to be in your fruits and vegetables. Under current rules, such pesticides subject us to a one-in-a-million risk of developing cancer over a lifetime. That represents a very small risk, it's true, but these chemicals may harm you in other ways—such as doing damage to your nervous system.

Of course, the best way to avoid these chemicals is to produce your own organic food—without pesticides or chemicals. That is rarely practical for most of us. Plus, growing your own food may not always guarantee uncontaminated produce. Chemical use in our society has become so ubiquitous that chemicals may already be present in your backyard soil even if you haven't put them there. Previous gardeners may have left residues on your property. Or if garbage or other wastes, unbeknownst to you, have been buried where you are growing your food, your crops may soak up harmful chemicals.

JUICE POWER

Buying organically grown produce can provide a measure of protection against pesticides, but even supposedly organic food has been found to contain small amounts of pesticide. Here again, it may not be the grower's fault—if soil and plants have been treated previously with pesticides, it may take years of chemical-free growing before these poisons disappear from the soil. So although the produce you are buying has not had chemicals applied to it, it still may have absorbed what's left over from the chemically dependent agriculture that was practiced previously on the land.

Pesticide Defense

In any case, you shouldn't let a fear of pesticides stop you from juicing fruits and vegetables. For one thing, fruits and vegetables are the high-fiber foods, rich in antioxidant vitamins that provide the highest level of cancer-fighting nutrients. Many nutrition researchers believe that a low-fat diet, high in fruits and vegetables, makes you less susceptible to most types of cancer. Consequently, high-fiber juices will lower your risk of being that unlucky one-in-a-million consumer who gets cancer from pesticide exposure.

Carl Lowe

And don't be fooled into thinking that fruits and vegetables are the only foods containing pesticides. If you decided to eat a diet of mostly meat and refined foods, you wouldn't lower your risk of pesticide exposure. You'd consume just as many—if not more—of these chemicals. For pesticides and other contaminants are also in fast foods like hamburgers and milkshakes as well as in steak and eggs. On top of that, considerable evidence exists to show that when you consume a diet emphasizing those kinds of high-fat foods, your immune system may be more vulnerable to cancer.

Safety Steps

With all that in mind, here are some steps you can take to minimize your risk from pesticides and chemicals in produce when you are making juices.

All produce should be thoroughly washed before being eaten or put into the juicer. The safest method is to apply soap and rinse them with warm water. Some special soaps are available for washing produce, but they are no more useful than regular soap.

Waxing of produce is more widespread than you may have thought. At the present time more then twenty varieties of fruits and vegetables are frequently waxed. These include: tomatoes, sweet potatoes, turnips, pumpkins, cantaloupes, apples, avocados, peppers, cucumbers, eggplants, limes, lemons, oranges, melons, parsnips, passion fruit, peaches, pumpkins, rutabagas, squash, pineapples, and grapefruit. Although there is a federal rule requiring stores to put up signs or labels indicating which foods have been waxed, the Food and Drug Administration has never enforced it.

If produce is waxed, it should probably be peeled before consuming. Scrubbing the surfaces of waxed produce will do you no good. Many waxes that are put onto food simply cannot be washed off no matter how hard you wipe. These substances are intended to make produce shinier and more attractive to shoppers as well as to kill molds and prevent dehydration. So they are impermeable to water.

That's why it is best to get rid of them. Many of these waxes—which are applied to everything from apples to cucumbers to tomatoes— are formulated with pesticides and fungicides and there is some evidence to show that they seal in other pesticides that have been applied to the food during growing.

According to the food companies and the government, there is little risk from ingesting these waxes. But for greatest safety, and if you have children who will be drinking your juices, waxed surfaces should be discarded. Several watchdog groups believe that children are especially vulnerable to pesticides.

If you are sure that produce has not been treated with wax or other chemicals, then you may want to leave the peel on when you juice your fruits and vegetables. Depending on the fruit, the peel can be a source of extra fiber. Frequently, too, many nutrients are contained just beneath the peel. And substances like vitamin C, which are destroyed by exposure to air and light, will be decreased by peeling.

However, you should never eat the rinds or peels of citrus fruits, melons, or cantaloupes. Often the outer surfaces of these fruits have been treated with fungicides and pesticides as well as coloring agents. For although many green oranges are ripe and perfectly good to eat, orange growers have found that people resist buying green oranges. So they frequently color their peels.

Recently, too, there have been reports of food poisoning from the salmonella growing on the outer surfaces of melons and cantaloupes. Salmonella is a dangerous, food-borne microorganism that can cause serious illness. It may sound silly, but even though you will not be eating the outside of melons and cantaloupes, they should be washed off before you cut them. Otherwise—and this has been documented— the inside of the fruit may become contaminated by salmonella transferred from the outer surface by the knife you use to cut it open. So wash before you slice.

In general, discard the outer leaves and surfaces of leafy vegetables, which are most likely to contain traces of pesticide. Studies show that celery often contains larger amounts of pesticide residues than do other vegetables, most of them concentrated in the leaves and tops. According to one report, cutting off and discarding the top of the plant will eliminate up to 90 percent of celery's pesticide residue. (The leaves often taste bitter and are unpalatable anyway.)

If your produce is organic, on the other hand, you may want to eat certain of these vegetable leaves since they are often the most nutritious. For instance, broccoli leaves actually contain higher levels of beta carotene and vitamins than the rest of the plant.

After you remove the outer leaves, wash everything else thoroughly. When you wash the inner part of a vegetable, be sure to rub the leafy surfaces to dislodge clinging dirt and don't forget to pull the sections apart to away any hidden debris.

It is also important to throw away any bruised or damaged parts of the plant, because plants usually produce toxins at such sites. In most cases, simply cutting away and discarding the discolored section is enough. One notable exception are potatoes that show evidence of shriveling. Studies have shown that discolored and wrinkled potatoes may have toxins throughout. So no part of a shriveled potato should ever be eaten.

You should also avoid buying produce that has been marked down because it has been in the store for a long time. The longer these foods are on the supermarket shelf, the fewer their nutrients. Many vitamins break down on exposure to heat, air, and light. So if produce hasn't been kept in a cool dark place, its nutrient content will be depleted.

That's also a reason you should not buy precut produce. Those cuts expose more of the fruits and vegetables to heat, light, and air. Plus, precut produce costs more. To keep vitamin content high, you should not cut up your produce until you are ready to pop it into the juicer.

Another point about bruises and damage: Some health-food proponents would have you believe that perfect-looking fruits and vegetables have been treated with heavy doses of pesticides or other chemicals. According to these self-appointed experts, organically grown plants are usually smaller and less healthy-looking than plants that have been doused with insecticides and growth promoters.

Of course, there is no evidence to support this claim. Yes, it is true that some untreated oranges look green instead of orange, that apples fall off the tree sooner if they're not fed alar (a growth promoter now banned in the United States), and that without a coat of fungicidal wax tomatoes may spoil faster. But that doesn't mean you should necessarily avoid good-looking fruits and vegetables. Organic produce can look terrific. And if it looks good enough to eat, it probably is.

Local and In Season

Besides shopping for organic produce, another step you can take to protect yourself against pesticides is to avoid imported fruits and vegetables or eat them sparingly. Unfortunately, foreign governments usually do not inspect their produce as carefully as the United States does (and even the U.S. regulatory agencies frequently undergo sharp criticism for lax inspection). In addition, other countries allow a wider range of pesticides to be used. Many of these chemicals have been found to be carcinogenic.

Some studies have found that up to two thirds of imported produce contain pesticide residues compared with only about one third of domestic produce.

Finally, even though U.S. officials occasionally spotcheck imported foods, these inspections are few and far between and many importers have found ways to circumvent them.

For these reasons, produce brought in from abroad generally carries a higher overall risk of chemical contamination than domestic food, although the risk is probably not very great. But if you want to be extra cautious in your juice consumption, you can limit your purchases of out-of-season imported foodstuffs, and know that to some degree you are probably also limiting your intake of pesticides.

At the same time, some experts say you should only eat domestic produce in season. The theory behind this is that out-of-season produce, even when grown domestically, needs more pesticide applications to help it survive.

Variety Is the Spice of Juices

Another way to play it safe against pesticides while ingesting a healthy range of nutrients is to drink a variety of juices rather than relying too heavily on one favorite. In this way, you lower your chances of always being exposed to any individual pesticide in one particular fruit or vegetable. This advice also makes good nutritional sense because it ensures that you will consume different kinds of fiber, minerals, and vitamins.

In the long run, drinking the juice of a

healthy variety of fruits and vegetables—as well as eating a high-fiber, low-fat diet—is your best defense against pesticides and other pollutants in the environment. For that is the kind of diet that is most protective against the cancer these chemicals may cause. Despite the proliferation of books, television shows, and magazine articles warning about these substances, there is little else you can do to defend yourself. Most of these chemicals are tasteless, odorless, and otherwise undetectable in your food. Often, not even the government food inspectors can perform tests that will turn up all of the possible carcinogens that have been added to our food and environment. But by drinking juice, you lower your changes of being victimized.

5

GUIDE TO FRUITS AND VEGETABLES FOR YOUR JUICER

APPLES

Along with pears, apples qualify as a versatile juice fruit, whose taste makes them generally suitable for a wide range of juices. Not many nutritionists are impressed with the nutrients in apples, but the fiber they contain—including a water-soluble fiber called pectin—is good for decreasing cholesterol and promoting the health of your heart. Apples also contain some vitamin C as well as potassium.

Although thousands of different kinds of apples grow around the world, the main types sold in the United States are the delicious, the McIntosh, Granny Smith, and golden delicious. All are available year round. Delicious and McIntosh apples are red, and the Granny Smiths are green. The Granny Smith variety is the most tart, the McIntosh tends to be tangy, while the other two types are generally sweeter.

When choosing any kind of apple, look for fruit that is firm, without soft spots or bruises. Ripe apples can generally be stored at room temperature for about a week.

Apples often are coated in wax that contains fungicides and other preservatives. If you are not sure whether or not the fruit you are buying has been waxed, ask the produce manager.

If your apples are waxed, you should peel them before putting them into the juicer. Waxes applied to fruits and vegetables cannot be washed off.

APRICOTS

Lately apricots have become fairly expensive because of difficulties in growing this fruit and their fragility, which makes them hard to transport without damage. Most apricots are processed or dried rather than sold fresh.

Apricots originated in Asia and were known as the "sun's eggs" for their brilliant yellow color, a result of their large beta-carotene content. It is also this surplus of carotenoids that gives the fruit its anticancer reputation. Some alternative-cancer-treatment centers extract chemicals from apricots for use with their patients; however, in the United States, such treatment is illegal.

When buying apricots, look for fruit that is firm and not overripe. But don't buy fruit that is very hard and not approaching ripeness. It will probably rot before becoming edible.

Apricots are extremely rich in beta carotene and fiber and have some potassium, vitamin C, and B vitamins.

ARUGULA

Arugula is a tangy addition to vegetable juice that also contributes the minerals calcium, potassium, and vitamin C. It is a member of the mustard family—as confirmed by its sharp taste.

Arugula is sold in the supermarket in bunches. Look for arugula that still has its dark green color. The larger the leaf, the more peppery the taste will be.

In many places, arugula is available all year

round. Refrigerate after buying and use it in juice within a week.

ASPARAGUS

Reputedly one of Julius Caesar's favorite vegetables, asparagus is an excellent source of fiber, some vitamin C, carotenoids, as well as the minerals iron, potassium, and calcium.

When buying asparagus, look for stalks that are bright green, with spears at the top that are pointed and packed compactly together. Plumper stalks tend to be more tender. This vegetable is generally available from early spring to early summer.

Since asparagus loses nutrients and flavor quickly, it should be refrigerated when you bring it home and used in the juicer within two days.

AVOCADOS

Avocados probably contain more fat than any other item found in the produce section of the supermarket. Luckily, this fat is not saturated fat, the kind linked to heart disease. Most of it is monounsaturated, the type that seems to promote heart health. However, the fatty avocado is still high in calories, even if it isn't linked to health problems.

Luckily, along with the fat, avocados possess some very healthy nutrients—beta carotene, potassium, niacin, and iron.

When buying, avoid avocados that are bruised. If you squeeze a ripe avocado, it should feel only slightly soft. Don't pick one that feels spongy. Unripe avocados can be left out to ripen at home. Once ripe, eat or juice within a day or two.

BANANAS

While some people consider the tomato a vegetable even though it's a fruit, few realize that the banana is actually a gargantuan herb, the largest grown on earth. The original varieties were bitter and filled with inedible seeds, while the most widely sold variety in today's supermarket is sweet. However, plantains, a greenish-yellow variety of banana, contain less sugar than other bananas and must be cooked before being consumed.

Today, among Americans, bananas are the most popular fruit and annual consumption has reached more than twenty-five pounds per person. Bananas also have a reputation as one of the most pesticide-free fruits since the thick peel keeps most chemicals out. The peel should never be eaten and certainly not juiced.

Bananas can be bought green and allowed to ripen at room temperature. Look for fruit that is free of bruises and not too soft. Plantains should be green and can be blemished.

Once bananas are ripe—they will turn yellow and little dark speckles will appear on the peel—they should be juiced within two or three days. If the bananas you buy in the supermarket darken rather than turning yellow as they ripen, they have been kept at too cold a temperature before you bought them. However, they can still be used for juice. Their sugary bland taste makes them an excellent ingredient in sweet juices since they won't interfere with the flavor from other fruits.

Bananas are a good source of potassium, have plenty of fiber, some vitamin C, and carotenoids.

BEETS

Beets are excellent juice ingredients because of their rich color and sweetness—ounce for ounce, they probably contain more sugar than any other vegetable. (Of course, if you want to go easy on the sugar, cut back on the beets in your juice recipes.)

Available year round, beets should be chosen that are dark, red, and smooth. The small ones are reported to be tastier and more tender than the large. They can be refrigerated for up to ten days.

Beets are relatively high in potassium and iron. Their green tops can also be used in juices.

BELGIAN ENDIVE

This vegetable is one of the most bitter—and expensive—salad greens. But for nutrition and taste, a little bit goes a long way. Not much endive is needed to convey its strong taste, and a little bit provides healthy amounts of the antioxidant beta carotene as well as the minerals iron and calcium.

Belgian endive is available practically year round. When buying this vegetable, avoid plants with green tips—they should be yellow. Make sure the heads of endive are crisp and plump with no sign of decay. Otherwise this herb may taste too bitter to juice. Plus, you're better off purchasing short, squat rather than long, thins heads.

BLUEBERRIES

Bluberries are sweet sources of the antioxidant nutrients vitamin C and the carotenoids. The carotenoids are the source of the fruit's color, but they also protect your cells against free radicals—metabolic by-products that may cause heart disease and cancer. This fruit also provides some iron and potassium.

Blueberries come in two types—the wild variety (small berries that grow close to the ground in bushes) and the farm variety. Some argue that wild berries taste better. Unfortunately, they are also wildly expensive since the berries must be picked by hand. You probably won't have access to the wild variety unless you know of some bushes nearby where you can pick them yourself. The larger type, the kind most frequently found at grocery stores, is not as sweet but is more affordable since it is harvested by machine.

Blueberries are generally available from late spring to early fall. Pick out plump, deep-colored berries. The wild ones may be a little paler.

At home, wash the blueberries, keep them in the refrigerator, and juice them within a day

or two. You can freeze them for longer periods
of time.

BROCCOLI

Broccoli, a cruciferous vegetable, is believed to
have been developed by ancient Romans, per-
haps as a hybrid from cabbage. (Later, cauliflower was developed from broccoli.) The
familiar form of broccoli most often sold at supermarkets is the Calabrese, which is available
all year, although it is most plentiful in the fall
and winter months.

Broccoli should have florets that are firm and
tightly packed. Yellow buds that are open
means the plant has been sitting in the supermarket too long.

Along with carrots, broccoli is an important
vegetable to include in your juicing plan because of its large share of important micronutrients. It contains healthy amounts of vitamin
C and carotenoids as well as B vitamins, plus
the minerals calcium and iron and a good dose
of fiber. The outer leaves are the highest in beta
carotene, but if you are concerned about pesticides on the plant, these should be discarded,
since they are most vulnerable to chemical contamination.

Be sure to wash broccoli thoroughly before juicing, since insects and dirt can lurk in its tightly packed buds. It should be kept in the refrigerator and juiced within a day or two of purchase or picking.

Broccoli and other cruciferous vegetables also contain indoles, which can block breast cancers and other cancers by inactivating the estrogen hormones.

BRUSSELS SPROUTS

A relatively recent arrival in the human diet, brussels sprouts—first grown in Europe during the 1200s—are part of the cruciferous vegetable family. They contain indoles, substances that counter the action of estrogen hormones that have been implicated in breast cancer.

Indoles also may speed the body's metabolism of certain drugs, so if you are on medication, check with your doctor before juicing cruciferous vegetables.

Brussels sprouts are usually available during the fall and winter, rarely in the summer. When shopping for this vegetable, choose ones that have not yet turned yellow or grown puffy.

Brussels sprouts can be refrigerated for a day or two. They should be briefly steamed or boiled before being added to vegetable juice.

Besides indoles, these sprouts are good sources of the minerals iron and potassium and they are rich in vitamin C and fiber.

CABBAGE

Cabbage and other cruciferous vegetables (including broccoli, brussels sprouts, cauliflower, kale, and mustard greens) contain indoles, cancer-fighting compounds that stop the action of the estrogen hormones that can cause breast cancers and other cancers.

Indoles also may speed the body's metabolism of certain drugs, so if you are on medication, check with your doctor before juicing cruciferous vegetables.

Cabbage is the oldest of the cruciferous vegetables and is believed originally to have been grown by the ancient Romans. Bok choy, a Chinese version of cabbage, is now widely available in American supermarkets.

Cabbage is sold all year round. Buy firm heads free of mold or decay with crisp leaves. Most cabbage can be kept in the refrigerator for about a week and half before juicing, but bok choy should be used within a day or two.

To avoid pesticides, the outer leaves of the cabbage—which are most exposed to chemicals—should be discarded.

Besides indoles, cabbage is a good source of the cancer-fighting carotenoids, vitamin C, and the minerals calcium and potassium. Bok choy contains more carotenoids that the other cabbages.

CANTALOUPES

Of all the fruits you can put in your juicer, cantaloupe is one of the richest in carotenoids, including beta carotene, the vitamin-A precursor that many studies have linked to cancer prevention. This melon is also very rich in vitamin C and contains a healthy amount of potassium. All of which makes juice made from this melon a better buy than the classiest sports drink endorsed by the highest-paid athlete. It tastes better, too, in many people's opinion, and it doesn't contain any artificial anything (as the commercials are fond of saying).

Cantaloupes are generally available during the warmer months until the fall. When picking over the cantaloupes in the supermarket, look for mottled fruit with marks that look like netting. Don't buy cantaloupes with smooth surfaces. The end of a ripe cantaloupe should be soft, not hard. Use your nose, too, in your inspection process: a good-tasting cantaloupe should smell good.

Caution: There have been reports of cantaloupes and other melons whose outside surfaces were contaminated with salmonella, a microorganism that can cause food poisoning. These bugs can be transferred to the edible part of the fruit when it is sliced. So scrub the outside of this fruit with soap and water as soon as you get it home. Do not cut into unwashed fruit. Never put the rind of the cantaloupe or any other melon in the juicer. Discard it instead.

CARROTS

Carrots are all-star vegetables because they contain large amounts of carotenoids, substances that have been shown to protect against cancer and heart disease. Carrots supply a heroic amount of beta carotene, a vitamin-A precursor that the human body converts to vitamin A. Of all the carotenoids, beta carotene has best established antioxidant, cancer-preventive effects. Additionally, carrots are rich in fiber.

It is believed that this rich source of carotenoids was one of the earliest foods and was a staple of the primitive diet. A root vegetable, the carrot has been cultivated since ancient times in Asia and southern Europe.

Carrots, which are available all year long, should be firm, not soft, without discoloration of the rich, orangy color. The green tops of the plant may also be eaten or juiced.

Carrots can be stored in the refrigerator for up to two weeks without any appreciable decrease in the carotenoid content. Aside from its health benefits, carrot juice—in combination with other vegetables or by itself—is considered one of the best-tasting juices.

CAULIFLOWER

Just as broccoli was developed from cabbage, cauliflower was originally bred from broccoli. The most common variety sold in the United States has a white central cluster of buds known as the curd. In Europe, green varieties are often consumed.

Cauliflower is sold all year round, but is most abundant in the fall. When buying this vegetable, check for discoloration or other signs of aging.

Like broccoli, cauliflower should be carefully washed before juicing. It should be refrigerated and juiced a day or two after purchase or picking.

Cauliflower, broccoli, brussels sprouts, and cabbage are members of a family of plants called cruciferous vegetables that seem to protect against cancer. They all contain indoles—compounds blocking the action of the estrogen hormones that have been implicated in breast cancer. Cauliflower is also a good source of fiber and vitamin C and contains healthy amounts of the minerals potassium and calcium.

Indoles also speed the body's metabolic processing of drugs. That means drugs are eliminated faster from the body when you drink these vegetables in your juices. If you are on medication, consult your doctor before including these vegetables in your juices.

CELERIAC

Although its name, appearance, and taste make some think that this vegetable is the root of the celery (it is frequently referred to as knob celery and celery root), celeriac is a separate plant.

And while this vegetable's taste is reminiscent of celery, its texture is smoother and its creamy flesh is only edible after the tough, outer coating has been stripped away.

Before improved refrigeration techniques and shipping, celeriac was widely available at fruit-and-vegetable stands. It can be stored for long periods and it travels well. Nowadays, more delicate produce has replaced it. In recent years it has made a modest comeback, but it is relatively expensive.

Celeriac is generally available year round except in early summer. When selecting this vegetable, press down on dark spots; they may reveal decay. At home, trim its shoots and green top and put it in the refrigerator.

Celeriac is a rich source of the minerals iron and phosphorus and is relatively high in sodium.

CELERY

Despite its crunchiness, celery does not contain very much fiber. It is mostly water with some sodium and potassium and small amounts of vitamin C and beta carotene.

The ancient Romans believed celery could prevent hangovers (some believe this is why Bloody Marys are served with celery.) Although it lacks the nutrient density of other vegetables, adding celery to juices makes them a little tastier because of the high sodium content. In fact, until the 1600s, celery was only used for seasoning.

Celery is available all year round. The most common type, Pascal, should be light in color, firm not soft. Avoid celery that bends easily or is discolored.

In warm weather, celery added to juice will help increase the water and electrolyte content.

Caution: Do not include the leaves or tops of celery in your juices and do not eat these parts of the plant. Studies have shown that when pesticide residues are present in celery—and celery more frequently contains quantities of these chemicals than most other vegetables— the largest proportion is concentrated in the tops of the plant and the leaves. Do not consume these sections.

CHERRIES

People all over the world have been eating sweet cherries for dessert for thousands of years. They provide ample amounts of beta carotene and potassium as well as some iron, calcium, and vitamin C.

Today, the United States grows most of the world's cherries—and Americans eat most of them, too. The Bing variety is considered the best-tasting, most useful type for juice; the juice of Bing cherries has a dark color, unlike some of the other kinds, and it is one of the sweetest available.

Unfortunately, Bing cherries are generally

only sold in markets only from around the end of May to July. When you buy them, make sure they are already ripe; once you get them home, they will only decrease in flavor. Juice them as soon as possible.

Fresh cherries should have their stems still attached, should be firm not flabby, should show no signs of decay. Cherries without stems have been sitting in the store too long.

CRANBERRIES

Most domestic cranberries are grown in Massachusetts and Wisconsin. Generally speaking, the cranberry beverages sold in supermarkets are not juice—they are "drinks," since they contain reduced amounts of cranberries and increased sugar and water to cut the strong taste of the berries.

When buying these berries, look for fruit that is plump and firm with rich, dark red color. Don't purchase berries that are overly soft or wrinkled.

For many years, people have consumed cranberry juice to treat urinary infections, and there is considerable scientific evidence demonstrating that cranberry juice does help cure these infections by acidifying the urine. (If you think you have an infection, you should still seek medical help.) On the other hand, sweetened, bottled cranberry drinks are too diluted to be of any use in urinary infections. They don't cause the urine to become acidic enough.

Cranberries can be stored for up to a week before juicing. Besides their usefulness for urinary problems, they are rich in fiber and contain potassium and vitamin C.

CUCUMBERS

Cucumber is another ancient vegetable that has been part of the human diet for thousands of years. A relative of the melon, it contains large amounts of water—which keep this vegetable "cool as a cucumber" even in midsummer. Recently, researchers have come to believe that some of the cucumber's lesser-known nutrients are effective heart-disease fighters.

Cucumbers are available throughout the year, but the peak season is from spring throughout the summer. When buying cucumbers, avoid very large ones—they are lest sweet. Avoid cucumbers that have soft spots or shriveled sections. At home, they can be refrigerated for about a week.

Many cucumbers are waxed, so this vegetable should usually be peeled before juicing.

Cucumbers contain a little bit of beta carotene and potassium. More important, they also are a source of sterols—a type of steroid that helps the body excrete cholesterol.

DANDELIONS

Those weeds sprouting on your lawn or through the cracks in your sidewalk are actually one of the richest sources of beta carotene in the plant kingdom. So you can pick dandelions off your front walk (as long as you don't spray with pesticides) and add them to your juice, if you can tolerate this plant's pungent flavor. Besides beta carotene, dandelions provide large amounts of calcium, vitamin C, and iron.

Dandelions, as any gardener will tell you, are mostly available in the spring, although they may persist through the summer, depending on where you live. Pick plants that look healthy. If you're harvesting your lawn, don't juice the plants that have already gone to seed. Pull those up and blow their seeds into the air to plant a new crop. Just don't puff in the direction of your neighbors' lawns if they're obsessed with the idea of a "golf green" lawn.

EGGPLANT

This strongly flavored vegetable will not be to everyone's taste in juice, so be judicious about whom you serve it to.

Eggplants are available in a wide variety of sizes and colors. The most popular is the purple-black variety.

Choose eggplants that feel smooth without soft spots, which may indicate an overripe interior. You can buy eggplant all year round, but the largest supply is in the stores in late summer and early fall.

Eggplants are rich in potassium and have a taste that some people love.

FENNEL

This licorice-flavored vegetable is more popular in Europe and the Orient than in the United States, but it is now available in many supermarkets. The most suitable part of this plant for picking is its large, white bulb that grows aboveground. Its white stalks and sharp-tasting leaves are usually discarded. (Sometimes the leaves are used as a spice.)

Also known as anise, fennel is most often in the stores from fall to early spring. When choosing fennel, look for healthy-looking, green leaves. Don't buy when the bulbs have soft spots or brown splotches. Store fennel in the refrigerator where you can keep it for a day or two.

The leaves of the fennel are very high in beta carotene, but they are too sharp tasting for many people. The rest of the plant also contains beta carotene, although not in great quantities. In addition, fennel contains some calcium.

GARLIC

Garlic has a long-standing reputation for healing. In support of this, several studies indicate that persons who eat large amounts of this vegetable have a reduced incidence of heart disease, though this has not been confirmed. Garlic contains an antibiotic called allicin.

The sulfur compounds in garlic are also believed to have health benefits. Research shows these substances may stop the disease-causing activity of some carcinogens and may help cells in a precancerous state return to normal functioning. Studies in Asia indicate that the residents of some regions who ate large amounts of garlic reduced their risk of cancer of the esophagus.

In addition, substances found in garlic have been found to reduce the dangers of blood clotting, lower serum cholesterol, and inhibit the growth of tumors.

Of course, because of its pungent aroma, most people prefer to consume garlic in small quantities. So you may not want to include too much of this in your vegetable juice.

GINGER

Ginger is a spice that can be used to perk up some of your vegetable juices. It is fairly strong, and a little bit goes a long way. Don't add too much until you know what amount you prefer.

Ginger is a root that is available in the supermarket at all times. It is generally cultivated in the tropics and shipped to the United States; much of the domestic ginger is grown in Hawaii.

Some have compared the appearance of ginger to a gnarled potato. When buying this root, choose younger plants by their glossy look; older roots will have thickened and hardened skin. Store ginger in the refrigerator, where it will keep for at least two weeks.

Of course, you can buy preground ginger to

add to your juices, but this lacks the oomph of the fresh-ground stuff.

GRAPES

Grapes are a versatile group of fruits, long used for raisins and wine as well as juice. In most juicers, you can use either seedless or seeded grapes for juice. The juicers should separate the seeds from the liquid—or you can pull the seeds out by hand before juicing.

Among the most popular grapes are the green Thompson seedless and the blue Concord; these grapes contain a little beta carotene, as well as some iron and potassium and a tiny bit of vitamin C.

The best time to buy domestic-grown grapes is from late spring through fall. Grapes from South America (which may be higher in pesticides) are sold from late winter through the spring.

Buy grapes that are plump and flavorful. They won't ripen when you get them home; they will only deteriorate. Juice them as soon as possible after purchase although you can keep them in the refrigerator for about a week.

GRAPEFRUIT

The grapefruit, a recent arrival to humanity's diet, first appeared in Jamaica or Barbados in the late eighteenth or early nineteenth century. Those original grapefruits are believed to have been a mutant strain of the pomelo, a bitter fruit that was brought to the western hemisphere in the 1690s. The name "grapefruit" refers to the fact that this citrus fruit grows in bunches that resemble giant groups of grapes.

Today, nine out of ten of the world's grapefruits grow in Florida, Texas, California, and Arizona. The best time to buy them is in spring and summer.

When you examine grapefruits, don't worry about discoloration. Color variations should not affect the flavor or quality. Grapefruits should feel springy and thin-skinned when squeezed lightly. But don't buy fruit with pointy ends or coarse skins.

Although the pink and ruby-red varieties do not differ from the yellow grapefruit in taste, they do contain a higher level of the cancer-preventing carotenoids—this is what gives them their extra color. All varieties of the fruit are high in vitamin C. Grapefruit should be stored in the refrigerator and juiced within two weeks of purchase. The rind, which may be waxed or treated with pesticides, should be discarded.

Grapefruit also contain terpenes, substances that limit the body's production of cholesterol and inhibit the action of some carcinogens.

GREEN BEANS

Green beans, string beans, and snap beans are all haricot beans, a descendant of the ayacotl. Ayacotl is an Aztec name for a plant eaten by Native Americans since prehistoric times. The "string" in the name refers to a time when a tough, inedible string grew along the length of each bean. Today's varieties are largely stringless. The "snap" in snap bean is self-explanatory, but remember, if they don't snap, they're too tough to eat.

These beans are available all year, although the supply increases in spring and summer. In picking out the best beans, try the snap test. No snap, no sale.

Green beans should be refrigerated as soon as you get them home, and eaten or juiced within two or three days.

Green beans contain some beta carotene and a smattering of the B vitamins and potassium.

HONEYDEW MELONS

Many people confuse honeydew melon with cantaloupe. But nutritionally cantaloupes are superior in carotenoids and ascorbic acid. However, that doesn't mean honeydews are nutritional slackers. This fruit has a fair amount of potassium and calcium as well as a good amount of vitamin C, even if it isn't as much as cantaloupes contain.

Like cantaloupes, these melons are also available in the warmer months. Their surfaces are smooth. When you press the blossom end, the part that grew out from the plant, it should be slightly soft.

Ripe melons should be stored in the refrigerator and juiced within a day or two. If you buy a melon that isn't ripe, keep it out and let it ripen at room temperature, then juice.

Caution: There have been reports of melons whose outside surfaces were contaminated with salmonella, a microorganism that can cause food poisoning. These bugs can be transferred to the edible part of the fruit when it is sliced. So scrub the outside of this fruit with soap and water as soon as you get it home. Do not cut into unwashed fruit. Never put the rind of cantaloupe or any other melon in the juicer. Discard it.

HORSERADISH

While few people will attempt to drink juice made from this pungent root vegetable, a little bit of horseradish can be added to vegetable drinks to give them more zing. Don't add too much. Most people grate horseradish rather than attempting to cut its tough flesh with a knife.

Horseradish is generally on supermarket shelves in the fall and spring. Its root should be a fairly consistent shade of white and unbruised. You can keep it in the refrigerator indefinitely.

JERUSALEM ARTICHOKES

Having nothing to do with the Middle East or with artichokes, this North American tuber was grown by Native Americans before the arrival of Europeans and was probably given its present name by seventeenth-century French explorers. Why they chose the name remains unclear.

Also known as sun chokes, this vegetable is not very popular and is not available at all supermarkets. Nutritionally, however, it is worth seeking out. It contains healthy amounts of the minerals of iron, calcium, and magnesium.

Jerusalem artichokes are generally available in the fall and winter. You should pick out plants that are firm and tan and display no signs of shriveling. After purchase, sun chokes can be refrigerated for few days. But once you strip their outer covering and expose the edible flesh, you should juice immediately.

KALE

Kale, a member of the cabbage family, is a nutrition all-star. It is a rich source of the carotenoids—those antioxidant nutrients that give this vegetable its deep green or purple color—and contains substantial amounts of the minerals iron and calcium, several of the B vitamins, and vitamin C as well as phosphorus and potassium.

Kale is in the supermarkets all year. Look

for broad, crisp leaves with strong color. Leave behind kale that has droopy, unhappy-looking leaves.

Kale can be kept in the refrigerator for two or three days. But for optimum nutrition, juice it as soon as possible.

KIWI FRUIT

Originally imported from New Zealand, but now also grown in California, kiwi fruit is very high in vitamin C; per ounce of fruit, it is one of the highest.

Originally called the Chinese gooseberry, it was renamed for the flightless bird that is the national bird of New Zealand.

This fuzzy fruit can be bought at the supermarket year round. Ripe fruit is slightly soft and should be refrigerated when brought home and juiced within three days. Firmer fruit can be left out to ripen and then refrigerated.

Before using in juice, you should taste a small amount. Some people may develop a mild allergic reaction to kiwi fruit.

KUMQUATS

In the United States, most kumquats are eaten in marmalade or jam, but this fruit—the smallest of the citrus fruits—has a distinctive flavor and a rich nutritional profile that makes it a worthwhile addition to juice.

This fruit is the one member of the citrus family that has an easily edible peel, so the entire fruit can be put into the juicer. It is very rich in beta carotene and the carotenoids as well as containing calcium and potassium and a fair amount of vitamin C.

When buying kumquats, look for unblemished fruit with a bright orange-yellow color. Don't buy kumquats that look green. This fruit is usually available from fall to late winter. If you buy kumquats before you're ready to use them, you can keep them in the refrigerator for a few days.

LEEKS

If you can't stand the tears and burning eyes that result when you slice onions, try the leek, one of the mildest onions available. Shaped like oversized scallions, leeks are also much sweeter than most other members of the onion family.

At the present time, leeks are more popular in Europe than North America, but they have been gaining in popularity over the past ten years. This vegetable is available at all times of the year, with only a slight dip in supplies during the summer.

When shopping for leeks, pick plants that you can bend slightly and leave behind those with yellowing or wilting tops. When you get the leeks home, wash them thoroughly—sand and dirt cling tenaciously to this vegetable. Some experts advise slicing the entire vegetable lengthwise and rinsing under a steady stream of water to clear off dirt. You can keep leeks in the refrigerator for about a week before juicing.

The nutritional benefits of leeks are similar to other onions—they contain some vitamin C and the minerals potassium, iron, phosphorus, and calcium.

LEMONS

The juice of this tangy citrus fruit is richer in vitamin C than any other member of the citrus family and therefore has some of the strongest antioxidant properties. Even before the official

British discovery that scurvy, a vitamin-C-deficiency disease, could be prevented among sailors by consuming citrus fruit, many captains gave their crews lemon juice.

Today lemons, which originated in the East Indies or Malaysia, are grown around the world. Its juice can't be easily consumed undiluted because the astringent taste is too strong. But juicing the lemon in combination with other fruits creates a tangy drink rich in vitamin C.

When choosing lemons, which are most plentiful during winter and early spring, look for fruit that is smooth-skinned and bright yellow. Stay away from lemons that are thin and shriveled.

Generally, lemons can be kept in the refrigerator for two weeks before being used in juice. Besides vitamin C, lemons contain some beta carotene and potassium. They also contain terpenes—cholesterol-lowering, cancer-fighting compounds.

LETTUCE

Lettuce is an example of a vegetable whose carotenoid and beta-carotene content advertises itself. Carotenoids are both an antioxidant vitamin and a pigment. So the darker the lettuce, the more of these cancer-preventing substances will be present.

Iceberg lettuce, which is nearly white in color or transparent, generally lacks beta carotene and the related carotenoids. The other, darker lettuces all have more of these substances. These include the "butterhead" lettuces such as Bibb and Boston, the leaf lettuces, and the "loose-headed" varieties such as Romaine lettuce.

When you purchase lettuce, the plants should look alive—as though freshly plucked from the ground. Avoid those with limp leaves that are falling off. Don't buy lettuce that has started to rot or wilt.

To avoid pesticides, discard the outer leaves of this vegetable and wash the remaining sections thoroughly, wiping each leaf to dislodge dirt and insects. Although lettuce will keep in the refrigerator, for the most nutritive value it should be consumed within two or three days of purchase.

Besides beta carotene and the carotenoids, the darker lettuces also contain calcium and iron. All lettuces are good sources of fiber.

LIMES

Limes are frequently mistaken for lemons, which they do, in fact, resemble. Some limes are smaller and more green than lemons.

In the 1790s it became official policy for British sea captains to feed sailors lime juice to prevent the vitamin-C-deficiency-disease scurvy. The choice of lime juice (which gave the British the nickname "limeys") over lemon was politically motivated. Lemons had to be imported from other countries while the British had control over areas that grew limes.

Since lime trees are more sensitive to the cold than lemon trees, their growth in the United States is restricted to southern California and Florida. Mexico exports much of its lime crop to the United States.

Limes are grown all year round. Larger supplies are available in the summer. When buying limes, choose ones that feel heavy with even skin. Don't buy those with soft spots or other signs of spoilage. Limes should be stored in the refrigerator, where they can be kept for about two weeks. As with all citrus fruits, the peel should be discarded.

As the British navy recognized, limes are excellent sources of vitamin C, although because of the sharp taste few people can drink the juice straight. It is best when blended with other fruit. This fruit also supplies potassium and terpenes that protect against cancer and heart disease.

MANGOES

Mangoes, most of which are grown in India, are an excellent source of carotenoids. Introduced to the western hemisphere in the 1700s, they have grown in Florida since the nineteenth century.

Use caution when peeling the mango. You may have an allergic reaction to the inside of the peel. Some people recommend wearing gloves while peeling.

When buying mangoes, check that they don't have gray or black spots. Avoid those that seem wilted. The shape and size of mangoes is not crucial. The fruit can weigh anywhere from a third of a pound to several pounds.

Keep mangoes at room temperature until they ripen and grow soft, then refrigerate and use for juice as soon as possible.

Besides beta carotene and the carotenoids, mangoes are high in vitamin C and potassium, and contain some calcium as well as magnesium.

MUSHROOMS

The most commonly found mushroom in supermarkets is the *Agaricus hisporus*—rather bland, white plants that are available year round. Pick ones that feel smooth and unshriveled and avoid ones that are damaged or slimy.

Mushrooms should be stored in the refrigerator, but not for more than a day or two.

Mushrooms have some iron and B vitamins as well as the electrolyte potassium.

NECTARINES

Nectarines have a bit of an identity problem. No one's sure if this fruit is a peach-plum hybrid, a peach without fuzz, or a distinct variety of fruit. But whatever its origin, golden-fleshed nectarines are generally rich sources of beta carotene and the carotenoids (the source of their golden color), which can protect you against heart disease and cancer.

Almost all of the nectarines grown in the United States come from California and are sold in supermarkets in the summer. Nectarines from South America are available in late winter and early spring.

Purists insist that the sweetest-tasting nectarines are ripened on the tree. But unless you live next to a nectarine orchard or you grow your own, you have to settle for those that have ripened after harvest. These are still not a bad choice for taste and nutrition.

At the supermarket, look for nectarines that are deep-colored, plump, and without obvious signs of damage. If they are firm, let them ripen at room temperature for a day or two before refrigerating. Once ripe, they can be kept cold in the crisper drawer for a few days before juicing.

ONIONS

Although onions are used sparingly in vegetable juices, their distinctive flavor adds a great deal of taste in small quantities. They also contain a fair amount of potassium, some vitamin C, and calcium.

Onions have been part of the human diet since the beginning of recorded history. There are five kinds grown in the United States—yellow, Bermuda, red, and green onions, as well as scallions.

JUICE POWER

The sweetest kind of onion is the red and this is most frequently added to juice. When buying onions, which are sold all year, look for solid bulbs without soft spots or decay. They should be covered with paperlike skins that pull away easily. Discard the outer leaves before juicing.

Onions can be kept in a dry, cool space for up to a month. But use them before they sprout.

Raw fresh onions are a health food. Unfortunately, today, many people seem to eat their onions fried or as part of fatty onion rings. The extra fat added during processing offsets the value of this nutritious vegetable.

ORANGES

Oranges are citrus fruits that have been used as a rich source of vitamin C for about two hundred years. To get adequate amounts of this vitamin (also known as ascorbic acid) you should include juice from the orange—or some other citrus fruit—every day.

Recent research has indicated that substances called terpenes in oranges and other citrus fruits may fight heart disease by inhibiting cholesterol production in the body. Terpenes may also stimulate the production of enzymes that prevent certain carcinogens from doing harm.

Carl Lowe

Additionally, oranges and other citrus fruits contain bioflavonoids, which some people believe help the body utilize vitamin C, although there is no scientific evidence to substantiate this claim. (Bioflavonoids are sometimes referred to as vitamin P.) Oranges also contain a good amount of potassium and a fair amount of beta carotene and carotenoids.

Because of its refreshing taste, as well as its contribution to good health, oranges have long been popular. The first oranges are thought to have been grown in China more than four thousand years ago. In the sixteenth century, Chinese oranges were first imported into Europe. At the time, this fruit was considered an aphrodisiac, although there is no scientific evidence to support this.

Today, oranges are grown in large quantities in warm climates. In the United States many oranges are shipped from Florida and California and imported from Brazil and Israel. The American crop of oranges is the largest in the world.

Navel oranges—without seeds—are in season from midfall to late spring. Temples are generally available during the winter. Hamlin and Parson Brown oranges are particularly well suited for juice and are in season in October, November, and December.

The best oranges to use in juicing are those that feel heavy and firm and have no soft spots.

Untreated Florida oranges tend to be greenish in color. To appeal to consumers, they are frequently artificially colored. Artificially colored oranges are supposed to be labeled as such, but this rule is most often ignored. Because of this treatment and the pesticides and fungicides applied to orange peels, these peels should always be discarded. Oranges should be kept refrigerated until used for juice. (Don't keep them around for more than a week or two.)

According to some reports, oranges picked late in the season have less vitamin C than those picked earlier. Valencias, a type often used to make frozen orange juice, may also have a little less vitamin C than some other varieties. There is no information available on the terpene content of Valencias.

PAPAYA

Originally a native of the western hemisphere, papayas are now grown around the world. Most of the fruit available domestically is grown in Hawaii. Many papayas are sold unripe and still green. When ripe, they become bright yellow.

Choose papayas that are firm and may be spotted—the skin doesn't have to appear blemish free. Store the fruit at room temperature until it takes on a yellow hue similar to a ripe banana. Then it can be refrigerated for a day or two before eating. (The seeds should be removed before eating or juicing.)

To ripen a papaya, some people slice into the peel without disturbing the flesh and stand the fruit upside down—i.e. wide-side up—in a glass for a day.

The mild-flavored papaya is high in beta carotene and vitamin C and also contains a good deal of potassium.

PARSLEY

Although often used merely as a garnish, parsley is a valuable dietary item that should be part of everyone's meals.

In ancient times, parsley was worn around the neck to ward off evil spirits. This herb also has a long history as a breath freshener and is used to mask the aftertaste of garlic, onions, and alcoholic beverages.

In modern times, researchers have discovered that parsley contains compounds called polyacetylenes, which inhibit the body's production of prostaglandins, hormones that, under certain circumstances, may promote cancer. In addition, polyacetylenes can counter powerful carcinogens such as benzopyrene, a result of pollution.

When buying parsley, which is available all year long, look for fresh-looking leaves that seem to have plenty of life left in them. Juice as soon as possible after purchase.

Besides polyacetylenes, parsley also contains beta carotene, potassium, vitamin C, calcium, and some iron. So a little bit of this herb goes a long way toward improving your health.

PEACHES

Originally a symbol of immortality in China, peaches are now grown all over the world. The two main types are freestones, which have a large central seed that is easily removed from the fruit's flesh, and the clingstones, which are harder to separate.

The peach season is from May until the early fall. When buying peaches, avoid fruit that is overly soft or firm. Very light, tan areas on the skin may mean the fruit has started to go bad.

Don't refrigerate peaches. Let them ripen at room temperature and then juice them immediately.

Peaches are very rich in carotenoids and are a good source of potassium. They are excellent for use in sweet juices, since their taste blends in well with other fruits. They are also high in fiber and they contain some calcium.

PEARS

Although pears are not particularly rich in any individual nutrient, their taste makes them a good, all-around performer in many different fruit-juice blends. Not that there are no nutrients in pear juice—it has small amounts of beta carotene, and vitamin C as well as a smattering of calcium and potassium—but its taste is more impressive than its nutritional credentials.

Pears are available in wide variety. The two most popular are the Bosc and the Bartlett. Usually, both of these are sold all year round. Bartletts should be bright yellow and unscarred. Bosc pears are more brown in color. Buy both varieties firm and unripe and then leave them out at home until they soften. Once ripe, they can be refrigerated, but it is better to juice them as soon as they are soft.

PERSIMMONS

To many people, an unripe persimmon is an inedible disaster. This fruit has to be extremely ripe to be sweet enough to eat. Otherwise it is bitter and astringent and will leave a bad taste in your mouth.

But if you know your way around a ripe persimmon (it has to be so ripe that it seems ready to rot), this fruit is sweet and tasty. Just make sure the skin looks shriveled up and ugly before juicing or eating—that's the sign of ripeness. Ripe persimmons contain healthy amounts of beta carotene, vitamin C, and potassium.

Persimmons are generally available from the middle of fall until the middle of winter. Look for bright persimmons whose stem caps are still intact. It's best to buy firm fruit and let it sit around the house until ripe—then refrigerate and juice within a couple of days.

PINEAPPLES

Although Hawaii is now known for this fruit, pineapples originated in North America and were not introduced to the Pacific island until the late eighteenth century. Pineapples have to ripen on the plant for the best nutrition and taste. They are sold all year round.

When buying this fruit, make sure the crown of leaves at the top looks fresh and healthy and that the pineapple has a strong, sweet smell. Signs of discoloration or dead leaves mean the fruit has probably started to go bad.

Ripe pineapples should be refrigerated immediately and used within a day or two for juice. The fruit contains substantial amounts of vitamin C and carotenoids.

Be cautious when introducing pineapple into your juices, some people may develop allergic reactions.

PLUMS

Most of the plums sold in today's supermarket are durable varieties that have been developed within the past century. Because of their versatility and adaptability, plums are grown all over the world, though most varieties originated in either Japan or Europe.

Plums of European origin include the dark purple El Dorado and the green-tinted greengage. When people speak of "prune-plums," or "fresh prunes," they are usually referring to plums of European origin. (A prune is a type of plum that has been dried.) Japanese plums tend to be larger and include the Santa Rosa, a red-colored fruit.

Domestically grown plums, mostly from California, are usually available toward the end of spring until midfall. During late winter, many plums are imported from Chile.

From a nutritional standpoint, plums add beta carotene to juice as well as potassium and a tiny bit of vitamin C.

When choosing plums, look for moderate-sized fruit of rich color. Avoid bruised fruit. It's best to buy them firm and let them soften at room temperature at home. Once ripe, juice them immediately or put them in the refrigerator for a day or two but not longer.

POTATOES

Before being used for juice, potatoes must be cooked. Do not consume raw potatoes at any time. They are best when baked.

The consumption of fresh potatoes, baked at home, has dropped by at least two thirds during the twentieth century. As a result, we no longer get the full benefit of the vitamin C, fiber, potassium, and other nutrients in this useful, fat-free vegetable. Even after baking, most of the potato's nutrients survive.

Unfortunately, at the same time as fresh potato consumption has dropped, the amount of processed potatoes we eat, such as fast-food french fries and potato chips, has multiplied by almost fifty times in recent years. And those processed potatoes that we're eating out of colorful cardboard containers and plastic bags have been stripped of many of their nutrients. In their place is the tasty fat added during frying, often accompanied by a hefty dose of salt. In many cases, preservatives are also applied to fried potatoes.

When buying potatoes, always avoid ones that are sprouted, bruised, or discolored. Especially avoid shriveled potatoes, which may contain very harmful toxins. These chemicals will not be eliminated by cooking.

Before baking, potatoes should be thoroughly scrubbed to remove caked-on dirt. Cut off sprouts and discard. Before putting in the juicer, the skin should be removed.

Besides its vitamin-C, potassium, and fiber content, a potato also contains a healthy amount of several of the B vitamins as well as protein.

PUMPKINS

Pumpkins are one of the richest sources of beta carotene and the other carotenoids as well as fiber. That combination—since carotenoids and fiber are anticancer foods—makes this vegetable a potent force in the dietary struggle against carcinogens in the environment. But if you're leaving your fiber in your juice, you can't add too much pumpkin to the beverage; it will make the drink too thick. Also, many people find pumpkin hard to digest, so you may want to cook it first before adding it to your juice.

Pumpkins are usually available in the fall, around the time of Halloween. When buying a pumpkin, look out for those that have started to rot. Avoid those that are bruised. When you get the pumpkin home, it can be kept for about a week in a cool, dry place. Don't eat the rind. But the seeds can be cooked in the oven when you use the meat in your juice.

Besides being full of beta carotene, pumpkins contain electrolytes (necessary for heart health) and some iron.

QUINCE

Not many people like to eat raw quince—it is too tart—so before purchasing a great deal of this fruit, sample one or two.

In medieval times, this member of the pear family was quite popular. Now it is mostly used in preserves. It contains some carotenoids and a modicum of vitamin C.

Quince is sold from the middle of summer to late fall. You should look for unbruised fruit of a bright yellow colors with no punctures or bruises.

One advantage of quince is its durability; it can be refrigerated for a long time before juicing. If you decide not to use it in juice, you can do as the Victorians did—hang it up as an air freshener.

RADISHES

Like carrots, radishes are a root vegetable usually available the entire year, though the supply frequently peaks during the spring. To

Americans, the most familiar forms of this plant are the red varieties, some of which have white tips. But a Japanese type—which is white and has a sharper taste—can also be found in supermarkets of large cities.

Radishes should be firm, without soft spots, and the color (when red) should be fairly bright.

Radishes have a fair amount of potassium and some vitamin C but, despite their outer color, contain hardly any carotenoids.

RASPBERRIES

Delicate and therefore difficult to ship and costly to buy, this fruit may be too expensive for most people to use in juice. Unless you live in a part of the country that grows raspberries, expect to pay a premium for them in the supermarket. They are usually available during the summer.

Despite their costliness, some people are hooked on the taste of raspberries and are willing to pay the price for them. Nutritionally, they are a good source of vitamin C, a fair source of carotenoid antioxidants, and contain potassium, iron, and calcium.

Raspberries are available in a variety of colors, including red, black, purple, yellow, and amber. Pick out fruit that is plump, undamaged, and free of mold. Don't buy raspberries that are stuck together. And don't assumed that a large price tag assures quality—raspberries are expensive no matter what shape they are in.

After buying raspberries, juice them as soon as possible. They won't last.

RUTABAGA

Sometimes known as a yellow turnip, rutabaga—which is larger and has a much stronger flavor than the turnip—is believed to be a mutant strain of the turnip family. Often this vegetable is coated with wax before it is sold in the supermarket. Be sure to peel this wax (you can't wash it off) before juicing or cooking.

Unlike turnips and squash, which taste better when they are small, the size of the rutabaga doesn't alter its taste or nutrition. Rutabagas are richer in beta carotene and vitamin C than turnips. They also contain substantial amounts of the minerals potassium and calcium.

At the grocery, pick out rutabagas that are firm and unbruised. They can be stored for a long time at room temperature as long as extremes are avoided.

SOUR CHERRIES

Although this fruit has been cultivated since the days of the Assyrians, today the leading cherry producer in the world is the United States. Michigan is the largest producer, followed by New York.

Sour cherries don't travel well. Their skin is delicate and they bruise easily. So don't be too picky. They are most abundant in summer.

For many people, sour cherries are an acquired taste. But those who love them love them ardently. Before including them in juice you are making for company, make sure your visitors are fans of this fruit.

Sour cherries are high in beta carotene and contain vitamin C and folic acid, which is important in the production of hemoglobin.

SPINACH

If spinach is popular with Popeye, it may be due to its healthy beta-carotene content. Spinach is loaded with this nutrient—ounce for ounce it has almost triple the amount of Romaine lettuce. Compared with iceberg lettuce, an ounce of spinach has two thousand times as much beta carotene.

But although spinach contains potassium, vitamin C, and calcium, this vegetable won't make you a woman (or man) of iron. For it contains oxalic acid, a substance that limits the human body's iron absorption.

Spinach also contains folacin, one of the B vitamins. Although many foods contain this substance, it is frequently destroyed during cooking. So when you drink juice made with raw spinach, you can be sure of consuming this nutrient. Folacin is used by the body for hemoglobin in the blood. Pregnant women deficient in folacin may suffer anemia or miscarry. Folacin deficiency can also result in birth defects such as spinal bifida.

Spinach was probably first grown in Persia. The most common type sold in the United States is the Savoy variety, which is available all year round. When buying spinach, be sure to purchase unwilted leaves with rich green color. Leave behind spinach that looks lifeless or damaged.

Spinach can be kept in the fridge two or three days before juicing. But be sure to wash it thoroughly before using. Usually it's best to soak it in water and carefully rub the dirt off of each leaf. Otherwise, clinging sand may accompany the leaves into your juicer.

SQUASH

The squash family consists of native North American plants that food historians believe may have been the first plants cultivated by native North Americans. Squash comes in a dizzying variety of shapes, sizes, and colors, but are classified into two large categories: the hard-skinned winter squashes and the thinner-skinned summer squashes.

Nutritionally, the winter squashes are superior. They generally contain larger amounts of beta carotene and the carotenoids—antioxidant nutrients researchers think may prevent cancer and heart disease. Squash also contains vitamin C, iron, and potassium.

The winter squashes (which include pumpkin) should have a consistent, unblemished shell. This variety, which includes acorn, butternut, and Hubbard squashes, may keep for at least three or four months without being refrigerated, as long as the room temperature stays around 70 degrees F.

The summer squashes, which include zucchini and yellow crooknecks, don't keep as well; they have to be refrigerated and used within days of purchase. When you buy this type, look for young, small squash without soft spots. Larger squashes are less sweet.

If you are talented in the garden, squash, particularly summer squash, is notoriously easy to grow.

STRAWBERRIES

Varieites of this popular fruit have been adapted to grow in almost all climates. As a result, they are generally available year round, although the supply expands during spring and early summer.

When you buy strawberries, make sure the green caps are still intact (though you should remove these before juicing) and make sure the berries are free of mold and soft spots. Strawberries should be refrigerated and juiced within twenty-four hours of purchase. For best taste, don't store this fruit more than two days in the refrigerator.

Strawberries are an excellent source of fiber and vitamin C.

SWEET POTATOES

Like regular potatoes, sweet potatoes must be baked before eating or putting them in your juice. Here, too, don't include the peel.

Sweet potatoes are extremely rich in beta carotene and fiber and also contain a healthy amount of vitamin C. They also contain calcium, electrolytes such as potassium, and about half the protein of a regular potato and some of the B vitamins.

When you purchase sweet potatoes, look for ones that show no sign of rot or bad spots. Do not refrigerate them, but use them within three or four days of purchase.

SWISS CHARD

Swiss chard, a relative of the beet, is grown for its leaves, not its root. That is why Swiss chard is also known as leaf beet.

This plant is generally available from spring through fall. It is popular among home gardeners because it survives the dog days of summer better than other vegetables such as spinach.

On the nutritional playing field, Swiss chard is strictly major league. It contains an impressive supply of the carotenoids and has a fair amount of vitamin C and potassium.

When buying Swiss chard, pick out crispy leaves and unwilted stalks. Refrigerate and juice within three days.

TANGELOS

With a name that sounds like a Latin dance, the tangelo is a relatively recent hybrid that comes in several varieties, all of which contain healthy amounts of vitamin C. The tangelo is a cross between tangerines or mandarin oranges and either grapefruits or pomelos (a type of grapefruit).

A popular variety in some parts of the world is the ugli fruit, a bumpy-looking fruit with a pleasing taste. The ugli fruit is grown mostly in Jamaica. Also popular are the Minneolas—a seedless variety, cultivated in Florida, that yields a tart juice. Reputedly, the Minneola is the most popular juice fruit among citrus growers.

Tangelos are generally available from October through early January. Buy fruits that are firm and unbruised and refrigerate; they will keep for about a week. Don't buy too many until you are sure you like the tart taste.

TANGERINES

If you're in a hurry for citrus-fruit juice, tangerines are just about your best bet—the peel comes off more easily than that of any other citrus fruit. In seconds, you can have a juice rich in just about every phytochemical known to scientists. (Phytochemicals are the nutritive, antioxidant substances in plants that protect us from cancer and heart disease.) In particular, tangerines are rich in the carotenoids and vitamin C.

Most domestic tangerines—technically a variety of mandarin orange—are grown in Florida, and are generally in the supermarkets from midfall to late winter. In early fall, the tangerines sold are imported from Mexico.

When buying, look for fruit with a strong orange color without signs of mold. Loose-appearing skin is okay, since the skin is normally not strongly attached to the fruit within. When you get the fruit home, refrigerate and juice within three days.

TOMATOES

Long a favorite juice ingredient, this fruit (some people consider it a vegetable) was once thought by Europeans to be poisonous. In northern parts of the United States, locally grown tomatoes are generally available in late summer. Otherwise, tomatoes of varying quality are available year round.

It is estimated that consumption of canned and processed tomato products has climbed at least 500 percent since the early part of the twentieth century. Since this kind of processing always degrades the nutrient content of fresh vegetables, chances are we're not getting as many health-giving substances from tomatoes as we used to when we ate more raw produce.

You should avoid buying waxed tomatoes, since the wax, which may contain pesticides and preservaties, cannot be washed off. Do not store tomatoes in the refrigerator. They will only ripen at room temperature. Once ripe, they should be juiced within a day or two, although after ripening, they can be refrigerated for a few days.

Tomatoes are a good source of carotenoids and vitamin C. They are very useful in juices with other vegetables that are not as sweet, since tomatoes will dominate and mask other tastes.

TURNIPS

Despite its reputation as a lower-class food, the turnip is a high-class nutritive vegetable, especially the greens, which contain significant levels of the antioxidants beta carotene and vitamin C and a healthy dose of calcium. (The rest of the plant contains these nutrients, too, but not in such impressive amounts.)

The most popular turnips in the United States are those with white flesh and green or purple leaves on top. These are in the supermarket all year, with a slight increase in supply and a drop in price during the colder months.

When you buy turnips, look for those that are not too large, but are firm and smooth. The tops should be unwilted. When you get them home, cut off the greens (which you should also juice) and refrigerate. It is best to juice them within a week.

WATERCRESS

Watercress is a delicate member of the cabbage family and, like the other cruciferous vegetables, contains indoles, nutritive substances that may prevent certain types of cancer and be instrumental is preventing colon polyps.

Of course, most watercress lovers don't eat it for its nutritional value—they're infatuated with its peppery, refreshing taste, which makes it a flavorful, perky addition to many vegetable juices.

Watercress is highly perishable. So beware of bunches that are starting to wilt and are not a vibrant green. When you get it home, refrigerate it immediately. Keep it in a plastic bag to make it last longer. But juice it within a day or two at the most. It is in the supermarket year round, with peak supplies in the warmer months.

Besides indoles, watercress contains the antioxidant nutrients beta carotene and vitamin C, and also has a good amount of calcium.

WATERMELONS

Watermelon's high water content usually keeps the interior cool on hot days. So after hot-weather exercise, juice made with watermelon will be a refreshingly tasteful pickup.

But coolness and taste aren't the only things watermelon juice has going for it. It also contains elcctrolytes—those minerals like potassium that you lose in perspiration—and it has a good amount of carotenoids (which give watermelon its rich, red color). Added to that is a fair amount of vitamin C.

When you buy watermelon, make sure the outside is smooth and unbruised. Uncut sections will retain more vitamins, but if you buy sections already sliced, look for fruit that is dark red. Those will contain more carotenoids than paler, unripe fruit, and they will taste better, too.

Most watermelon is available in the summer and early fall. It should be stored in the refrigerator. Cut sections should be juiced as soon as possible. Whole watermelons should be used within a day or two.

Although no cases of salmonella (microorganisms that often cause food poisoning) have been reported on the exterior of watermelons, there have been instances of contamination of other types of melons. So scrub the outside of this fruit with soap and water as soon as you get it home. Do not cut into unwashed fruit. If you cut open unwashed fruit, harmful microorganisms on the surface may be accidentally transferred to the flesh of the fruit. Never put the rind in the juicer. Discard it.

6

CONSUMER GUIDE TO BUYING A JUICER

In the recent past, homemade juicing was for health nuts, and juicing machines were only available at health-food stores or via mail order. All that has been changing as more people seek out vegetarian foods and become concerned with eating healthier diets. At the same time, because of the growing popularity of juicing, the price of juicers has decreased and their availability has increased. You can walk into almost any department store or discount outlet and find juicers. And you'll find customers lined up to buy them, too.

Of course, many of the people buying juicers for the first time don't know that much about them or how they function. If you fall into this category, don't be intimidated. These machines are fairly uncomplicated and straightforward. In most juicers, the central mechanism is a spinning blade that cuts up the produce and lets the juice drain into a container; the fiber is either thrown into a separate container or filtered from the machine.

Generally speaking, you can judge most juicers by their price tags. The more you pay, the sturdier the machine and the higher its capacity. The most popular ones are, as you probably expect, electric. But if you want to make juice by hand, manual juicers are also available.

Don't be too nervous about picking out your first juicer. You can even get one for under fifty dollars to try out juicing and then graduate to a bigger machine when you are more knowledgeable.

For many people, a blender will be sufficient to begin their juicing odyssey. (Is there anyone who doesn't know what a blender is? It's simply a container with an electric-powered blade at the bottom that cuts up fruits, vegetables, and whatever else you drop in.) The key disadvantage to making juice in a blender is the fact that it doesn't filter out any pulp. As far as your health is concerned, that's good. The fiber in the pulp has important functions in the human body. It acts as a laxative that promotes the well-being of your gastrointestinal tract and lowers your risk of cancer and heart disease.

But many people find large amounts of pulp unpalatable. However, you can strain out some of the pulp with a sieve or strainer.

You can also buy a special, high-powered blender whose blade works in two directions. In a conventional blender, the blade always spins in the same direction. In this more expensive, two-directional machine, the blade constantly reverses direction at high speed so that the pulp is minutely granulated and is therefore less evident, although still present, in the final juice.

One warning: The makers of these high-powered blenders sometimes recommend putting everything connected to the plant into the blender—skins, seeds, stems. The machine pulverizes all of this material to a smooth, drinkable blend. However, some parts of the fruits and vegetables should not be consumed no matter how pulverized.

For instance, produce is frequently waxed with glossy substances containing pesticides and preservatives. Fruits and vegetables treated with these substances should be peeled before juicing. Also, the peels of citrus fruits are often colored and treated with fungicides you should avoid. And some leafy vegetables should have their outer leaves removed before juicing, since these parts of the plant have a greater likelihood of pesticide contamination than others.

In addition, while the seeds and stems of fruits probably won't hurt you if they are included in your juice, there is no evidence to show that they're good for you either. Better to dispose of them.

Centrifuging the Pulp

In most juicers, fruits and vegetables come into contact with spinning blades that allow the juice to flow into a collector while the pulp is spun off into its own "basket." In some machines, you have to remove this basket to clean the juicer. In others, the pulp is fed out of the machine.

Some people find machines that feed the pulp out to be a convenience; you don't have to stop the machine periodically if you are processing a large amount of juice. But in a well-made machine without a pulp "ejector," it is a relatively simple matter to pause, take the pulp basket off, and remove the collected fiber. Plus, automatic pulp removers can be noisy and they present one more mechanical element subject to malfunction. As a general rule, the fewer the moving parts in any machine, the less repair it will eventually require.

Some of the more high-priced machines do

not separate pulp from juice centrifugally, but push it through rotating blades that extract extra juice while ejecting pulp. Some of these machines can also be used for making your own peanut butter and ground grain.

For those who want to make juices by hand, the simplest devices available are those designed for citrus fruits. Some of these are simply cone-shaped, ribbed wedges upon which you press the halves of oranges, grapefruits, lemons, etc. In mechanized versions of this simple device, you press down upon a ribbed extractor powered by electricity that spins as you apply pressure. In other hand juicers, a lever allows you to apply added force to the fruit as the juice is squeezed out.

Available for those reluctant to pay money to the electric company to power plug-in juicers are machines that operate similarly to meat grinders. These machines slowly grind up the produce as it moves through a series of blades in much the same way as hamburger is ground. These machines are slow and many people find them tedious and tiring. But, as we said, they consume no electricity.

Features to Look for in Juicers

When picking out your machine, be sure to
check how easy it is to clean. The larger the
number of parts and the more difficult the dis-
assembly, the more discouraging it will be to
use the device. If the basket and blades allow
easy removal of pulp and fragments of food, it
will be that much easier to make juice. Nooks
and crannies that snag hard-to-remove pulp
pieces should be avoided.

Check the warranty on the machine. Some
of the larger and more durable devices are guaranteed for two years or more. On the smaller
machines, a one-year guarantee is the rule.

Safety may also be a concern if the machine's
entry port is too large. Although larger orifices
allow bigger chunks of produce to be fed to the
machine, they also make it easier for unwary
fingers to approach the blades. Narrow, long
entrances to the juicing chamber are safer.

Remember, *you should never stick your fingers into an operating juicer*. Your juicer should
come with a stick or other device for pushing
the food into the machine. You should also
never disassemble an electric juicer without
unplugging it. And don't wash the part of the
juicer that houses the motor assembly. Most

machines—after being unplugged—can simply be wiped with a damp cloth.

A dustcover for your juicer is another useful option for when you won't be using your machine for an extended period of time. Even if your machine is sold without one, you can improvise by placing a piece of plastic over the juicer when it is not in use. Otherwise, you may have to clean dust from the machine before making juice.

7

JUICE RECIPES

Although you should use these recipes as a general guide to making your juices, do not feel constrained by this list. While a juice composed of only one ingredient is frequently as tasty as any blend, improvisation on your part will certainly pay off as well.

And don't forget: While brands of bottled juices are generally uniform in taste, your own juice recipes will vary according to the characteristics of the available ingredients. Not all apples, for instance, are of equal sweetness or ripeness, and this will affect the final taste of the juices containing that fruit. You may find this fluctuation disconcerting. But to many of us, such surprises are a virture.

CRANBERRY JUICE COCKTAIL
½ **pound of cranberries**
½ **pint of strawberries**
½ **cantaloupe**

Wash fruits thoroughly. Wash the outside of the cantaloupe with warm soap and water before slicing to eliminate possible salmonella contamination. (For more information on salmonella, see the entry for cantaloupe in chapter 5.) Do not juice cantaloupe rind. Cut off green tops of the strawberries and discard. Juice ingredients.

This recipe adds sweetness to cranberry juice, which for most people is too bitter to drink alone. As an alternative, add some honey to cranberries juiced without the other ingredients. Stir in just enough honey to make the beverage palatable.

Benefit: Drinking cranberry juice has been shown to help alleviate urinary-tract infections. However, if you have a serious problem, you should still seek medical help.

VEGETABLE WAKE-UP
   1 head of broccoli
   1 bunch of celery
   3 large tomatoes
   4 brussels sprouts
   3 large carrots
   ½ onion or bunch of scallions
   2 sprigs of parsley

Wash ingredients thoroughly. Discard leaves and tops of celery (which may contain pesticides). Trim scallions or discard outer leaves of onion, trim broccoli, and then juice ingredients. Add pepper to taste.

Benefit: Cruciferous vegetables such as broccoli contain indoles, which can possibly lower your risk of some cancers.

ORANGE GRAPEFRUIT SIPPER
6 large oranges
2 medium grapefruits

Peel the fruit and juice. Discard the rinds, which may be artificially colored and treated with pesticide.

Benefit: Citrus fruits are a major source of vitamin C (ascorbic acid), an antioxidant vitamin that helps prevent heart disease and cancer. Fresh homemade juice contains more of this nutrient than the store-bought variety.

ORANGE TOMATO JUICE
6 oranges
2 tomatoes

Wash the tomatoes, peel the oranges, and discard the rind. Juice ingredients.

Although most people wouldn't ordinarily combine tomatoes and oranges, their tastes complement each other. This makes an excellent morning beverage.

Benefit: Both fruits contain significant levels of the antioxidant nutrients vitamin C and beta carotene, which help fight cancer and heart disease. Citrus fruits, such as oranges, also contain phenolic acids and flavonoids—substances that also act in the body as antioxidants.

ORANGE BANANA SUPREME
   6 medium oranges
   3 medium bananas
   ½ cup of strawberries

Wash the strawberries and trim the green tops. Peel the bananas and oranges and discard the rinds (which may be artificially colored and contain pesticides). Juice ingredients.

Benefits: Although sports drinks claim to replenish minerals lost during exercise, this drink supplies more than adequate amounts of those substances—known as electrolytes. This drink contains a healthy dose of potassium, a mineral important to keeping blood pressure down and the heart muscle behaving properly. It also contains magnesium, important for proper bone growth.

PUMPKIN GRAPEFRUIT JUICE
 2 cups of pumpkin meat
 2 medium grapefruits

Scrape pumpkin from its shell. Peel the grapefruit and discard the rind. Juice ingredients.

Benefit: If you use pink grapefruits in this recipe, you will have a juice super rich in beta carotene, an antioxidant nutrient that helps color grapefruits pink and pumpkins yellow. This substance, one of the carotenoids, has been shown to be instrumental in preventing cancer and stopping the buildup of cholesterol plaque in arteries.

GAZPACHO JUICE
- 3 medium tomatoes
- 1 garlic clove
- 2 cucumbers
- 2 red peppers
- 2 limes
  Tabasco sauce (optional)

Wash the tomatoes. Peel the garlic clove and discard outer skin. Peel the cucumbers if waxed and discard peel. Wash the red peppers, cut open, and discard the seeds. Peel the limes and discard the rinds. Juice ingredients. Add Tabasco sauce to taste.

Benefit: Unlike many conventional gazpacho recipes that contain oil, this low-fat concoction is low in calories as well as being high in vitamin C and potassium, an important mineral lost during hot-weather exercise. Its tangy taste makes it an excellent breakfast drink for the "morning after."

RE-LEAF REFRESHER
- 6 brussels sprouts
- 2 cucumbers
- 3 celery stalks
- 1 head of romaine lettuce
- 1 head of broccoli
- ½ head of cauliflower
- 1 bunch of spinach

Wash and trim ingredients. If cucumbers are waxed, peel and discard (wax may contain pesticides). Trim celery and discard tops and leaves (which may contain pesticides). Juice ingredients.

Benefit: This beverage contains a large supply of beta carotene, an antioxidant that helps prevent heart disease and cancer and also has some vitamin C. The drink also contains iron, but the oxalic acid, present in the spinach, inhibits absorption of this material.

POTATO PIZZAZZ
   3 baked potatoes
   3 baked sweet potatoes
   2 cups pumpkin meat (uncooked)

Wash the potatoes and sweet potatoes thoroughly before baking. Scape pumpkin meat from inside of pumpkin and discard the rind. Juice all ingredients.

Benefit: This unusual juice is rich in beta carotene and other carotenoids, antioxidants that can prevent cancer as well as heart disease. It also contains phosporus, which helps in bone formation; potassium, an electrolyte important for healthy heart function; and some vitamin C, another antioxidant.

DOCTOR CARROT-PEP
   6 **medium carrots**
   2 **red peppers**
   1 **green pepper**
   ½ **head of broccoli**

Trim and wash ingredients. Cut open peppers and discard seeds. Juice ingredients.

Benefit: The carrots, which dominate the taste of this juice, also dominate in nutrition. They are rich in beta carotene, an antioxidant that gives carrots their orange color and can help prevent cancer and heart disease. The peppers and broccoli also supply beta carotene as well as some calcium, vitamin C, and the electrolyte potassium.

CARRIAGE JUICE
 6 medium carrots
 2 cabbage heads

Trim and wash carrots and cabbage. Juice ingredients.

Benefit: This beverage is a potent source of beta carotene, mostly from the carrots and indoles from the cabbage. Both of these nutrients have been shown to help prevent cancer. In particular, indoles have been linked to lower incidences of stomach, rectal, and lung cancer. This juice is also high in potassium. The fibrous pulp left over from this juice is particuarly tasty served with rice. It contains a high amount of soluble fiber, which can reduce serum cholesterol.

EVER-RED SPRITZ
½ **watermelon**
4 **medium pears**
½ **cup strawberries**
1 **bottle of seltzer (optional)**

Wash and trim the green tops from the strawberries. Slice the pears and discard seeds and inner core. Cut the flesh out of the watermelon and discard the rind. Juice ingredients. To make a carbonated drink, add seltzer.

Benefit: With the seltzer, this makes a sparkling drink containing more healthful vitamins, minerals, and other nutrients than almost any store-bought beverage. It is rich in vitamin C, contains a fair amount of beta carotene and the other antioxidant carotenoids, and has enough potassium—an electrolyte lost in sweat during hot weather exercise—to rival any commerical sports drink. Try this drink with kids who usually insist on the real "real thing."

CARROT-ORANGE ZINGER
 6 medium oranges
 6 medium carrots

Wash and trim the carrots. Peel the oranges and discard the seeds and the peel (which may contain pesticides, wax, and artificial color). Juice the ingredients.

Benefit: This combination provides a potent dose of antioxidant nutrients that can fight cancer and heart disease; oranges are high in vitamin C and carrots are high in beta carotene. The fiber filtered out of this beverage by most juicers is also healthy and tasty—since both fruits are very sweet. Much of this fiber is the "soluable" type, the kind that lowers blood cholesterol. Easy on the fiber, though. A little goes a long way and too much may cause gastrointestinal distress.

RADISH TANGO
   6 **medium radishes**
   2 **medium cucumbers**
   1 **tomato**
   1 **head of cabbage**
   1 **medium beet**

   Wash all ingredients. Trim the cabbage and discard outer leaves. Wash beet—its greens can be included in the recipe. If cucumber is waxed, wash and peel. Discard the peel. Juice ingredients.

   Benefit: This sharp-tasting juice contains some vitamin C, carotenoids, potassium, and iron. The beet supplies the iron and the vitamin C in the tomato helps your body absorb this mineral.

APPLE-PEAR PERKER
 4 large apples
 4 large pears
   cinnamon (optional)

Wash ingredients, core, and peel, discarding peel if the fruit is waxed. Juice the ingredients. Sprinkle cinnamon on top if desired.

Benefit: This juice contains some vitamin C and potassium. The fiber filtered out by most juicers is especially sweet and can be snacked on. It is full of soluble fiber, which may lower your blood cholesterol.

BANANA RULIUS
 4 medium bananas
 1 pint of blueberries
 ½ cup skimmed milk

Wash the blueberries. Peel the bananas and discard the peel. Juice the fruit. Blend skimmed milk with juice.

Benefit: This rich-tasting juice is an excellent summer beverage. It supplies plenty of potassium, a mineral lost during hot-weather exercise, and has a healthy dose of vitamin C as well as some iron and beta carotene. The vitamin C helps the body absorb iron.

MELONTONIC BABY
   4 medium apricots
   ½ cantaloupe or melon

Cut up the apricots and discard the pits. Wash the melon or cantaloupe with warm water and soap before cutting open. (The outside may be contaminated with salmonella. See the section on cantaloupe in chapter 5.) Cut out the flesh of the cantaloupe or melon and discard the rind. Juice the ingredients.

Benefit: This drink is rich in the antioxidant nutrient beta carotene as well as potassium. If you use cantaloupe, the drink will also be high in vitamin C. Both of these nutrients help prevent cancer and heart disease.

TURNIP SIP
  1 **bunch of white turnips**
  1 **bunch of spinach**
  1 **bunch of dandelion greens (optional)**
  ½ **clove garlic**

Wash and trim turnips, but do not discard the greens. Soak and wash spinach thoroughly. Peel outside leaf of garlic. Juice ingredients.

Benefit: While the strong taste of this juice will not appeal to everyone, it contains a good amount of calcium as well as the antioxidant vitamin C. If you use the dandelion greens—which have a very strong, characteristic taste—you also add a significant amount of beta carotene.

SCALLION SKIPPER
   3 bunches of scallions
   2 medium tomatoes
   1 bunch of spinach
   2 small carrots
   ½ head romaine lettuce

Wash all ingredients—soak the spinach and be sure to get all the sand off. Trim the carrots and scallions. Discard outer leaves of lettuce, which have the most chance of containing pesticide residues. Juice ingredients.

Benefit: This is another strong-tasting vegetable beverage that is not to everyone's taste. Others will find the flavor invigorating. It contains some vitamin C, a healthy dose of the cancer-preventing carotenoids, as well as some calcium.

LEMONY ORANGE-LIME PRIZE
   3 lemons
   4 limes
   5 oranges
   ¼ pineapple
   2 tablespoons honey (optional)

Peel the limes, lemons, and oranges. Discard the peels and seeds. Cut open the pineapple and remove one quarter of the flesh. Juice ingredients. Add honey if desired.

Benefit: The vitamin-C content of this beverage is very high. It also contains substances called flavonoids and phenolic acids, which may help to prevent cancer and heart disease.

CRANFRUIT FLIP
   2 oranges
   ¼ pint cranberries
   ½ banana
   ½ teaspoon grated nutmeg
   1 tablespoon honey (optional)
   ½ cup skimmed milk

Peel the oranges and discard peel and seeds. Wash the cranberries. Peel the banana and discard peel. Juice the ingredients. Blend milk with juice. Add honey if desired. Sprinkle on nutmeg.

Benefit: Calcium, vitamin C, carotenoids, and the electrolyte potassium make this drink a healthy, late-night refresher without the traditional alcohol content of a conventional flip.

PINKY'S BERRY JUICE
- ½ **pint of blueberries or cherries**
- 1 **banana**
- 3 **oranges**
- 4 **grapefruit (pink are better)**
- ¼ **pint cranberries**
- 2 **tablespoons honey (optional)**

Wash the berries or cherries and cranberries. Peel the banana and discard the peel. Peel the oranges and grapefruit and discard peel (which may contain pesticides and artificial color). Juice ingredients. Add honey if desired.

Benefit: The pink grapefruit in this concoction contains large levels of beta carotene, an antioxidant that supplies the pink color. This beverage is also high in vitamin C and potassium and has phenolic acids and flavonoids, antioxidants that may prevent cancer.

CUKEY'S COMESTIBLE
   2 cucumbers
   6 limes
   1 orange
   1 handful mint leaves
   2 tablespoons honey (optional)

   Peel cucumber (if waxed) and discard peel—
otherwise merely wash. Peel limes and orange
and discard peel (which may contain pesticides
and artificial color). Juice ingredients. Add
honey if desired.

   Benefit: Cucumbers contain nutrients
known as sterols, a type of steroid that helps
the body excrete cholesterol. In addition, this
beverage is high in the antioxidant vitamin C
as well as other antioxidants, which may prevent cancer and heart disease.

TOMATO SPARKER
  1 lemon
  3 medium tomatoes
  ½ teaspoon grated horseradish
  1 celery stalk
  ½ garlic clove
  3 tablespoons yogurt

Peel the lemon and discard peel (which may contain pesticides). Wash the tomatoes and celery. Trim tops and leaves off celery (parts of the plant that are most often the sites of pesticide residues). Peel outer leaf from garlic clove. Juice ingredients. Add yogurt to juice.

Benefit: This perky drink has a fair amount of vitamin C. It also contains a good supply of potassium, an electrolyte lost during hot-weather exercise.

MILK FROTH
2 medium pears
2 medium apples
½ cantaloupe
2 medium bananas
½ pint strawberries
1 cup of skimmed milk

Wash the outside of the cantaloupe with warm water and soap before slicing to prevent contamination of the meat with salmonella that may be present on the outside. (See section on cantaloupe in chapter 5.) Scoop out cantaloupe meat and discard peel. Wash the pears, apples, and strawberries. Trim and discard green tops of the strawberries. Peel the bananas and discard peels. Juice ingredients. Blend milk in juice.

Benefit: In contrast to a standard milkshake, this froth is low in fat with a healthy dose of calcium and antioxidants, including vitamin C and the carotenoids. The leftover pulp, which contains cholesterol-lowering fiber, is also tasty and can be served with yogurt.

SWEET BEET DRINK
4 **carrots**
3 **medium beets**
1 **head romaine lettuce**
2 **oranges**
2 **apples or pears**

Wash and trim carrots. Trim beets. Core apples or pears and peel if waxed (wax may contain pesticides and cannot be washed off). Peel oranges and discard peel, which may contain pesticides and artificial coloring. Wash romaine lettuce and discard outer leaves. Juice ingredients.

Benefit: The high sugar content of both beets and carrots gives this drink its sweet taste. It has a large amount of beta carotene, some potassium, iron, and vitamin C, which increases the amount of iron you absorb from this beverage.

WHEATIE SMOOTHIE
1 lemon
2 pears
3 apples
2 bananas
3 tablespoons wheat germ

Peel the lemon and discard peel which may contain pesticides. Wash and core pears and apples. Peel if they are waxed (The wax contains pesticides and cannot be washed off.) Peel the banana and discard the peel. Juice ingredients. Add wheat germ to juice.

Benefit: Adding wheat germ to this recipe increases its vitamin E content. This vitamin is an antioxidant which may help prevent certain types of cancer. This drink also contains the electrolyte potassium as well as vitamin C. The sweet pulp that is separated from the juice may be eaten straight or with yogurt. Its water soluble fiber lowers blood cholesterol.

Carl Lowe

HOT SIDER
  4 **medium apples**
  ½ **pineapple**
  2 **lemons**
  2 **oranges**
  2 **pears**
    cinnamon to taste

Peel apples and pears if waxed (wax cannot be washed off). Wash and core apples and pears. Discard seeds. Peel and core pineapple. Peel lemons and oranges, discard peels. Juice ingredients. Gently heat on stove. Cinnamon can be added to individual servings to taste.

Benefit: Conventional hot apple cider is tasty and refreshing on a cold winter day, but it lacks vitamins and minerals. This tangy substitute contains vitamin C and the carotenoids as well as electrolytes. Once again, the leftover pulp contains a hefty amount of fiber. Heat the fiber in the microwave and pour it over ice cream or ice milk (which is lower in fat than ice cream). The water-soluble fiber can lower blood cholesterol.

APPLE DIMPLE
 3 **medium apples**
 1 **celery stalk**
 3 **medium carrots**
 1 **lemon**

Wash apples. Peel if waxed (wax cannot be washed off). Trim celery and discard tops and leaves, which may contain pesticides. Wash and trim carrots. Peel lemon and discard the peel. Juice ingredients. Add more lemon if you like your juices on the tangy side.

Benefit: Contains some vitamin C, plenty of beta carotene, and some potassium. Also contains flavonoids, which may help to prevent cancer.

ALMOST-INSTANT BREAKFAST DRINK
3 medium bananas
2 pears or apples
1 orange
1 cup skimmed milk
2 tablespoons brewer's yeast

Wash and peel apples or pears if waxed. Core apples or pears and discard seeds. Peel bananas and discard peel. Peel orange and discard seeds and peel (which may contain artificial color and pesticide). Juice ingredients. Add skimmed milk and brewer's yeast to juice. You may want to vary the amount of brewer's yeast in this recipe. Some people find its taste too strong in large quantities.

Benefit: This beverage makes a nutritious low-fat breakfast that contains healthy amounts of calcium, vitamin C, B vitamins, and potassium. If you're not in too much of a hurry, down a tablespoon or two of the leftover pulp, which contains water-soluble fiber that lowers blood cholesterol and may also help keep your blood pressure down. (Plus, this fiber is just about calorie free.)

SPINACH SPINNER
2 cups spinach
5 stalks medium asparagus
½ head of broccoli
   basil and pepper to taste

Wash the spinach thoroughly to remove dirt. Trim and wash asparagus and broccoli. (Outer leaves of broccoli may contain pesticides. If the broccoli was organically grown, retain outer leaves, since these are high in beta carotene.) Juice ingredients. Add spices to taste.

Benefit: This spicy drink is high in beta carotene and contains vitamin C and some calcium.

ESSENCE OF BORSCHT
   6 beets
   1 lemon
   ½ head of romaine lettuce
      pepper to taste

Wash and trim the beets (leave some of the greens intact). Peel the lemon and discard the peel and seeds. Wash the lettuce and discard outer leaves, which are more susceptible to pesticide contamination. Juice ingredients. Add pepper or other spices to taste.

Benefit: This cold drink contains beta carotene, some iron as well as flavonoids, phenolic acid, and vitamin C: antioxidants that may prevent cancer and cardiovascular disease.

VICHYSSOISE LITE
  2 **baked potatoes**
  ½ **onion**
  1 **bunch of scallions**
  ½ **head of broccoli**
  1 **cup of skimmed milk**

Scrub the outside of the potatoes before baking. Remove outside leaves of onion. Wash and trim scallions. Wash broccoli and discard outer leaves to avoid pesticides (although the outer leaves are the most nutritious—if the broccoli is organically grown, include these in the recipe). Juice all ingredients. Blend skimmed milk into juice.

Benefit: Although no one would mistake this for a conventional vichyssoise, this version is much lower in fat (it is virtually fat free) and contains healthy levels of vitamin C, beta carotene, and calcium.

WATERCRESS-ASPARAGUS SPECIAL
 1 bunch of watercress
 6 asparagus spears
 2 medium carrots
 ½ head of romaine lettuce

Wash the watercress and lettuce. Discard lettuce outer leaves to avoid pesticides. Wash asparagus and carrots, trim carrots. Juice ingredients.

Benefit: Watercress is high in vitamin C and beta carotene and contains some iron (your absorption of the iron is enhanced by the presence of vitamin C). The other ingredients help boost the beverage's beta-carotene level and also contribute potassium.

BOK CHOY CHUG-A-LUG
   3 stalks of bok choy
   ½ head of cabbage
   4 beets

Wash and trim the beets, leaving some of the greens intact. Wash the cabbage but dispose of outer leaves to remove portion of possible pesticide residue. Wash and trim the bok choy. Juice the ingredients.

Benefit: Bok choy is rich in beta carotene as well as vitamin C. This drink also contains indoles, substances that are believed to help prevent cancer.

AVOCADO ARDOR

- 2 large avocados
- ½ head of romaine lettuce
- 1 stalk of bok choy
  pepper to taste

Wash avocado, cut open, discard pit, and scrape out meat. Clean the romaine lettuce and dispose of outer leaves to avoid pesticides. Wash and trim bok choy. Juice ingredients. Add pepper or other spices to taste.

Benefit: Although avocados are relatively high in fat for a vegetable, the fat is mainly monounsaturated, a variety of fat that is believed to lower blood cholesterol. Avocados are also high in carotenoids, antioxidants that protect your cardiovascular system and protect you from cancer. They also have healthy amounts of iron and potassium.

PEACHY KEEN
6 **medium peaches**
2 **medium pears**
2 **large bananas**

Wash the peaches, cut them open, and dispose of the pits. Wash and core the pears. Peel the bananas and dispose of the peel. Juice all ingredients.

Benefit: Peaches contain some beta carotene as well as potassium, which is also supplied by the bananas in this recipe. The cholesterol-lowering pulp from this recipe is tasty by itself or may be eaten with rice or yogurt.

MOCK MINESTRONE JUICE

 2 tomatoes
 ½ head of cabbage
 1 clove of garlic
 ½ head of broccoli
 6 brussels sprouts
 3 sprigs of parsley
 1 onion or stalk of scallions
   pepper and oregano to taste

Wash the cabbage and discard outer leaves. Peel garlic. Wash broccoli and discard outer leaves. Wash parsley, brussels sprouts, tomatoes, and scallions (if used). If using onion, peel off outer leaves. Juice ingredients. Add spices to taste.

Benefit: Making a beverage with a wide variety of vegetables gives you the benefits of many antioxidants, which can help prevent cancer and cardiovascular disease. Many of these substances—some of which scientists refer to as phytochemicals—have nutritive benefits that have not yet been fully explored. But researchers believe these substances will be shown to help prevent cancer and heart disease.

CREAM GREENS
  2 cups of spinach
  6 asparagus spears
  5 brussels sprouts
  1 cup of skimmed milk
    pepper and spices to taste

Wash spinach thoroughly. Wash sprouts and asparagus spears. Juice all ingredients. Blend skimmed milk with juice. Add spices to taste.

Benefit: While "cream" soups contain a great deal of saturated fat, using skimmed milk with the juices can give them a creamy feel—by mixing in air and making the concoction frothy—without adding fat. Cutting dietary fat by substituting drinks like this for their fatty alternatives can greatly aid your health (fat in the diet adds calories and high-fat diets have been blamed for cancer, obesity, and heart disease). This drink also contains antioxidants, potassium, and calcium.

PRUNISH

 6 pitted prunes
 1 orange
 ½ lemon or lime
 ½ cup skimmed milk
 1 tablespoon honey (optional)

Peel orange and lemon or lime and discard peel, which may contain artificial color and pesticides. If prunes are bought prepitted, check to make sure pits are out. Juice all ingredients. Blend milk with juice.

Benefit: Well known for their laxative effects, prunes are also rich in iron. They also have some beta carotene and vitamin C, as do oranges, lemons, and limes. This drink is a very sweet way to get a high dose of fat-free calcium. It is best made in a blender rather than juicer, to retain all the fiber of the prunes. If you make it in a juicer, the leftover fiber will be an effective laxative (and is believed to help prevent colon cancer).

CREAMSICLE DRINK
2 oranges
2 medium bananas
8 ounces vanilla-flavored fat-free yogurt
   or plain yogurt with teaspoon of
   vanilla extract and ¼ tsp. of honey

Peel oranges and discard peel and seeds. Peel bananas and discard skins. Juice all ingredients. Blend yogurt with juice.

Benefit: This drink, which tastes creamy because of whipped bananas, is high in calcium, vitamin C, and other antioxidants. When it is made in the blender, the retained fiber (which most juicers will filter out) will make the drink even creamier.

PLUM NOG
5 medium plums
3 medium bananas
½ cup skimmed milk

Wash plums and dispose of pits. Peel bananas and discard skins. Juice all ingredients. Blend skimmed milk with juice.

Benefit: This drink is a low-fat dessert that supplies potassium, calcium, and beta carotene. Drink it on New Year's Eve and it's guaranteed not to give you a hangover.

JUICE 'EM HIGH
2 medium tomatoes
1 celery stalk
1 onion or scallion stalk
8 ounces of nonfat yogurt

Wash tomato, celery, and scallion (if used). Trim celery and discard tops and leaves, which may contain pesticides. Peel outer leaves of onion (if used). Juice all ingredients. Blend yogurt with juice.

Benefit: This beverage provides a good dose of nonfat calcium along with vitamin C and carotenoids and potassium.

MUSHROOM WITH A VIEW
6 large mushrooms
1 stalk celery
1 cup buttermilk

Wash mushrooms. Wash celery and trim, discarding leaves and tops, which may contain pesticides. Juice ingredients. Blend buttermilk with juice.

Benefit: Although you have to be a real mushroom lover to go for the taste, this drink contains healthy amounts of iron and B vitamins. Buttermilk is a low-fat source of calcium, while the celery contains some vitamin C and beta carotene.

RASPBERRY PREMIER
1 pint of raspberries
1 orange
1 medium banana
1 tsp. vanilla extract
8 ounces of nonfat yogurt

Wash the raspberries. Peel the banana and discard the peel. Peel the orange and discard seeds and peel. Juice ingredients. Blend yogurt and vanilla extract with juice.

Benefit: This thick dessert is easy to mix in the blender and provides vitamin C, beta carotene, and calcium. It is virtually fat free.

PAPAYA PIZZAZZ
   2 papayas
   ¼ medium watermelon
   2 medium bananas

Wash papaya and remove seeds. Wash watermelon with soap and water before slicing. Scrape out flesh and remove seeds. Peel bananas and discard peels. Juice ingredients.

Benefit: This refreshing fruit drink is rich in beta carotene, vitamin C, and potassium, all important nutrients for cardiovascular health.

STRAWBERRY MILK
   1 pint strawberries
   ½ lemon
   1 cup skimmed milk

Wash strawberries. Trim and discard green tops. Slice lemon in half. Juice strawberries. Blend in skimmed milk. Squeeze several drops of lemon juice into individual servings to taste.

Benefit: This makes a tasty, low-fat source of calcium. It is preferable—and easy—to make this in a blender so that you retain all of the heart-healthy fiber from the strawberries. This drink is also high in vitamin C.

CELERYBRATE
   4 medium carrots
   1 celery stalk
   1 sprig of parsley
   ½ head of broccoli

Clean the celery and dispose of leaves and tops, which may contain pesticide residues. Wash parsley and broccoli. Juice ingredients.

Benefit: This simple beverage supplies beta carotene, potassium, and some calcium. The broccoli also contains sulforaphane, a substance that stimulates the body's production of anticancer enzymes.

CARROT'S POP
   6 medium carrots
   ½ head of cabbage
   ½ head romaine lettuce

Wash carrots, cabbage, and lettuce. Discard outer leaves of cabbage and lettuce, which may contain pesticide residue. Juice ingredients.

Benefit: Antioxidants and other cancer-preventing substances are abundant in this simple vegetable drink. Cabbage, a cruciferous vegetable, contains indoles, substances that have been linked to a lower incidence of cancer.

ORANGE-GRAPE PUNCH
2 medium oranges
1 bunch of seedless grapes

Peel oranges, discard peel, which may contain coloring and pesticides. Discard seeds. Juice ingredients.

Benefit: This drink has plenty of vitamin C as well as the electrolyte potassium. Studies have shown that potassium has protective effects on the cardiovascular system.

MS. GREEN
4 sprigs of parsley
1 stalk of celery
1 head of broccoli
3 stalks of asparagus
1 tomato
½ cup of spinach

Clean the celery and dispose of leaves and tops, which may contain pesticide residues. Wash and juice all other ingredients.

Benefit: This juice contains a wide range of cancer-preventing substances including indoles, which are believed to protect against colon cancer.

THE BERRY SPECIAL
1 pint raspberries
½ pint strawberries
1 pint blueberries

Wash all ingredients. Trim the green tops off the strawberries and discard. Juice ingredients.

Benefit: Although any of these berries make excellent juice on their own, many people like to drink a blend, varying the proportions according to their preferences. This beverage supplies a heavy dose of vitamin C, which is believed to prevent cholesterol from forming plaque on artery walls.

CALL OF THE FLOWERS
  1 head of cauliflower
  ½ cup dandelion greens
  ½ head of cabbage
  3 beets

Wash all ingredients. Dispose of outer leaves of cabbage, which may contain pesticides. Juice all ingredients.

Benefit: While the taste of this drink, which includes the distinctive flavor of dandelions, may turn some people off, it contains a hefty dose of beta carotene and other carotenoids and indoles, both of which are believed to be strong anticancer nutrients.

NECTAR DELIGHT
 4 medium nectarines
 1 orange
 1 bunch of grapes
 1 banana

Wash and pit nectarines. Peel orange and banana and dispose of peel, which may contain coloring and pesticide. Wash grapes. Juice ingredients.

Benefit: While many people depend on store-bought orange juice for their daily dose of vitamin C, homemade juices are richer in this antioxidant. And this drink also includes a good supply of beta carotene—much more than you'll find in plain orange juice.

THE PRODUCE BLOSSOM SPECIAL
2 beets
2 medium carrots
1 stalk of celery
2 medium apples
2 medium pears

Wash celery and dispose of tops and leaves, which are more likely to contain pesticide residue. Wash other ingredients, pit the apples and pears. Juice ingredients.

Benefit: Besides carotenoids, this drink also includes pectin (which will be well represented in the leftover pulp—have a spoonful). Pectin may stop the spread of lung cancer.

CHERRY UPPER
1 pint of cherries
2 tangerines
1 pear

Wash and pit the cherries. Peel the tangerine and discard the peel and seeds. Juice ingredients.

Benefit: This drink is another source of vitamin C as well as potassium.

WATERMELON CRUSH
¼ small watermelon
½ pint of strawberries

Wash strawberries, trim and discard green tops. Remove flesh of the watermelon. Remove seeds. Juice ingredients.

Benefit: This drink serves up a whopping dose of beta carotene and vitamin C—both of which can help keep your arteries clear. The electrolytes in this drink should also help control your blood pressure.

KALE AWAY
1 bunch kale
2 tomatoes
½ head romaine lettuce

Wash ingredients. Discard outer lettuce leaves, which may contain pesticide residue. Juice ingredients.

Benefit: This drink contains sulforaphane, which stimulates the production of anticancer enzymes.

SWEET SPOT
2 medium carrots
1 head cauliflower
2 medium apples

Wash ingredients. Pit the apples. Juice ingredients.

Benefit: Population studies show that when you consume these types of vegetables every day (in your juice and on your dinner plate), you reduce your chances of a wide range of cancers including colon cancer.

JUICE BREATHER
  1 head of broccoli
  ½ clove of garlic
  2 cucumbers

Peel outer layer of garlic and discard. Peel cucumbers if waxed (pesticide-containing wax cannot be washed off) and discard peel. Wash broccoli. Juice ingredients.

Benefit: This pungent juice contains nutritive substances that have been shown to keep down triglycerides—fats in the blood.

ARUGULA ARTISTRY
  1 bunch of arugula
  3 beets
  2 pears

Wash all ingredients. Pit the pears. Juice ingredients.

Benefit: This beverage delivers beta carotene in a big way as well as vitamin C and a fair amount of calcium.

APPLE COT
   3 apricots
   2 medium apples

Wash fruit and remove seeds. Juice ingredients.

Benefit: This drink includes the anticancer nutrients beta carotene and pectin.

CITRUS OF CELERIAC
   1 celeriac root
   2 lemons
   2 tomatoes

Peel celeriac (discard peel). Peel lemons and discard peel and seeds. Wash tomatoes. Juice the celeriac flesh and other ingredients.

Benefit: This strong-tasting juice includes vitamin C and the minerals iron and calcium.

TOMATO PUNCH
1 stalk of celery
1 stalk of scallions
1 orange
1 tomato
1 sprig parsley

Wash tomato and parsley. Cut off and dispose of celery tops and leaves, which may contain pesticide residue. Peel orange and dispose of peel, which may contain coloring and fungicide. Wash and trim scallions. Juice ingredients.

Benefit: This drink contains polyacetylenes, which inhibit the body's production of prostaglandins, hormones that have been linked to cancer.

CUTE JUICE
2 cucumbers
2 stalks of scallions
1 tomato

Peel cucumbers if waxed (wax cannot be washed off). Wash and trim scallions. Wash tomato. Juice ingredients.

Benefit: This drink is a good source of sterols—types of steroids that help the body excrete cholesterol.

VEGETABLE SPICER
1 tomato
1 sprig parsley
4–6 sage leaves
1 red pepper
1 stalk celery

Wash all ingredients. Trim tops and leaves of celery and discard since these may contain pesticide residue. Juice ingredients.

Benefit: This tasty beverage is a potent blend of antioxidant nutrients, which protect the body against cancer and artery blockages. It also contains a fair amount of potassium and some calcium.

THYME TO WAKE UP
¼ cup fresh thyme
3 carrots
2 apples
1 scallion

Trim scallion. Wash apples, carrot and thyme. Take out apple seeds and discard. Peel apple if waxed; wax cannot be washed off. Juice ingredients.

Benefit: This drink does what its name says—its sharp taste will wake you out of an early-morning funk or jolt you back to your senses in the evening. It contains a solid dose of beta carotene, potassium, and vitamin C. You can cut back on the thyme, which has a very strong flavor, without noticeably affecting the nutrient content.

TOMATO TOPPER
2 tomatoes
1 baked potato
½ pint of strawberries

Wash strawberries, trim and discard the green tops. Wash the tomato. (Wash potato before baking.) Juice ingredients.

Benefit: This interesting blend of fruit and vegetable makes a nutritious addition to a quick breakfast (you can make the juice the night before and store in the refrigerator). Although it may contain a little less vitamin C than a comparable glass of orange juice, it probably includes more beta carotene and also has a fair amount of potassium.

SWEET BABY
1 orange
½ cup rutabaga

Peel orange and discard peel, which may contain coloring and fungicide. Peel and slice rutabaga. Discard peel. (Most rutabagas—also known as yellow turnips—are waxed. This wax cannot be washed off; it must be peeled.) Juice ingredients.

Benefit: This beverage also offers a tasty alternative to that repetitive glass of orange juice you may be drinking every morning. The turnips not only give that same old drink a new taste twist, they also add beta carotene, vitamin C, and some calcium.

KIWHIP
4 kiwi fruit
2 apples
1 pear

Wash ingredients. Discard apple and pear seeds. Juice ingredients.

Benefit: Kiwis are a rich source of vitamin C, an antioxidant that protects the cardiovascular system. This juice also includes some pectin (it is in the pulp as well), a type of fiber that protects against cancer.

PINE ELOPE
½ pineapple
½ cantaloupe
10–12 seedless grapes

Wash cantaloupe with soap and water to remove possible salmonella contamination. (See cantaloupe entry in chapter 5.) Slice cantaloupe, discard seeds, and remove flesh. Peel and core pineapple. Wash grapes.

Benefit: This drink is extremely high in beta carotene, vitamin C, and potassium, all of which protect your cardiovascular system.

GINGER TONIC
1 pineapple
1 orange
1-inch piece of ginger root

Peel and core pineapple. Peel orange and discard the peel, which may contain artificial coloring and fungicide. Juice ingredients.

Benefit: This beverage also makes a good breakfast drink and includes plenty of vitamin C and other phytochemicals—anticancer nutrients that are provided by citrus fruits.

POTUMKIN
1 baked sweet potato
1 cup pumpkin flesh
1 lime

Peel lime and discard peel (which may contain pesticides). Wash sweet potato before baking. Slice open pumpkin, remove seeds, and measure out one cup of flesh. Juice ingredients.

Benefit: This drink contains a healthy dose of beta carotene and other carotenoids, antioxidants that help your immune system fight off free radicals and prevent cancer and heart disease.

MR. GREEN BEANS

- 1 cup of green beans
- ½ head of broccoli
- 1 stalk of asparagas
- ½ head of romaine lettuce
- 1 summer squash

Dispose of outer leaves of lettuce, which may contain pesticide residue. Wash and juice ingredients.

Benefit: This beverage is very high in beta carotene and indoles, which are believed to help prevent cancer.

IMPROVE YOUR HEALTH!

___ **THE FAT-TO-MUSCLE DIET** Victoria Zak, Cris Carlin, M.S., R.D., and Peter D. Vash, M.D., M.P.H. 0-425-12704-4/$4.50
Fast, safe, permanent weight loss with the revolutionary diet plan that boosts your calorie burning power!

___ **THE 200 CALORIE SOLUTION** Martin Katahn, Ph.D. 0-425-09668-8/$3.95
From the author of The Rotation Diet—how to burn an extra 200 calories a day and lose weight!

___ **THE GOLD'S GYM WEIGHT TRAINING BOOK** Bill Dobbins and Ken Sprague 0-425-10404-4/$4.99
From the most celebrated gym in America—the fast, scientific way to shape your body beautifully.

___ **BEYOND DIET: The 28-Day Metabolic Breakthrough Plan** Martin Katahn, Ph.D. 0-425-09915-6/$4.50
Beat the diet game by changing your body metabolism in just 28 days . . . and eat more than you ever thought you could!
